Student Workbook

The New Professional Chef™

Fifth Edition

The Culinary Institute of America

Student Workbook

The New Professional Chef™

Fifth Edition

VNR VAN NOSTRAND REINHOLD
New York

Contents

Introduction

Cooking is a practical art. Each of the hundreds of thousands of recipes that you might find in cookbooks is based on some fundamental principles, which *The New Professional Chef* attempts to uncover. A thorough understanding of these points, including ratios to achieve proper thickening, sanitation and safety practices, or purchasing and quality standards, make up an important part of your training. Key terminology and the general procedure for preparing a variety of foods *can* be learned from a book. The intention of this workbook is to help you use *The New Professional Chef* in the most effective way possible. Theory is important, especially when it is paired with practical experience.

There is no substitute for hands-on learning in this field, but there is also no need to hamper yourself by being uncomfortable with the language that is spoken in professional kitchens. As you complete the chapters in this workbook, you should become familiar with a wide range of subject areas that are of concern to the chef.

We begin with the history of the foodservice profession, and move on to learn about sanitation, safety, nutrition, equipment, and product identification. Then our attention is turned to the ways that meats, poultry, and fish are cut in the kitchen to suit the needs of a restaurant's menu. Once these fundamental skills are introduced, the actual preparations such as mirepoix and bouquet garni are explained, followed by chapters devoted to a variety of cooking methods, such as preparing stocks, soups, sauces, and a wide variety of techniques used to prepare entrées and side dishes. The book concludes with sections devoted to the pantry and the bakeshop.

Cooking is a combination of skills. Some can be learned only through hands-on experience and plenty of time spent in a kitchen, working directly with foods. The more often you can actually grill a steak, sauté a piece of fish or chicken, or prepare a rice pilaf, the more comfortable and familiar you will become with the process. Eventually, it will become second nature. You might even find yourself chuckling over a novice's attempt to sauté too many veal cutlets in a pan that is too small, or wondering why on earth the salad person doesn't realize that it is absolutely essential to remove every drop of water from the greens.

Stay humble, however. There will always be some "fine point" that you haven't had the chance to learn yet, or a cut of meat or a type of fruit that you have never seen before. The process of learning about food and cooking goes on constantly throughout one's career.

Chapter 1

Introduction to the Foodservice Industry

This chapter is intended as a very brief introduction to the foodservice industry. We read about several different topics, all of which have had an effect on the current status of our industry. Key areas such as general history, politics, travel, exploration, and science have played important roles. We need to see this industry as a part of the rest of the world. We must also learn to appreciate our work as being valuable. The title of chef is one that should be used with pride.

After reading and studying this chapter, you should be able to:

1. Discuss the changes that have occurred throughout history. Many of them have had a direct influence on the way we cook today.
2. Recognize and name some of the key historical figures who were important to the foodservice industry. Their work and the contributions they have made are a part of everything that we do today.
3. Recognize and name some major figures in cooking today. These are the people known by the public for their work in changing the way we cook, the way we eat, the kinds of ingredients we use, and the way restaurants are designed.
4. Discuss and describe the changes in our own families, in the workplace, and in the world that are influencing the trends and fads throughout the foodservice industry.
5. Name many of the different jobs that are open to anyone interested in pursuing a career in the foodservice industry. The potential to find a special job that meets an individual's talents and lifestyle is greater than might be expected.

Matching

1. __G__ M. Boulanger
2. __D__ Fernand Point
3. __A__ Anne of Austria
4. __E__ Brillat-Savarin
5. __B__ La Varenne
6. __F__ Escoffier
7. __C__ Carême

a. Wife of Louis XIII, member of the Hapsburg family.

b. Author of *Le Vrai Cuisinier Francais* (published in 1651).

c. The man responsible for creating a system known as the "grande cuisine."

d. The man who opened the first restaurant (as we known them today).

e. Author of *The Physiology of Taste*.

f. Author of *Le Guide Culinaire*.

g. Chef credited with laying the foundations for nouvelle cuisine.

Multiple Choice

1. The brigade system is
   a. used to assign specific duties in the kitchen and to make the work organized and efficient.
   b. a nautical term used to describe the parts of a ship.
   c. rarely used today.
   d. often confused with the merit system.

2. Which of the following individuals are known for their food writing?
   a. Julia Child.
   b. Craig Claiborne.
   c. James Beard.
   d. All of the above.

3. Which of the following foods are remnants of the time that the Moors were the rulers in Spain?
   a. Sweet syrups.
   b. Pickles.
   c. Oats.
   d. Rye bread.

4. Vacuum packaging, freeze drying, and irradiation are all examples of
   a. cooking techniques.
   b. fast foods.
   c. processing and packaging techniques used to keep foods wholesome longer.
   d. illegal practices in California.

5. Which of the following foods were not introduced to Europe from the Americas?
   a. Turkey.
   b. Chocolate.
   c. Potatoes.
   d. Melons.

6. Increased acceptance of Italian, French, and German foods were probably the result of
   a. boredom with traditional American dishes.
   b. World Wars I and II.
   c. the publication of a number of special cookbooks.
   d. increased immigration to the United States from these countries during the 1950s.

7. The French Revolution was important to the history of the foodservice industry because
   a. the army trained many new cooks and chefs.
   b. the wealthy noble families were encouraged to hire more people to work in their kitchens.
   c. chefs from the noble families were afraid of being killed if they remained in France, so they left the country and opened their own restaurants.
   d. the revolution established a new respect for haute cuisine.

True/False

1. _F_ The head waiter is responsible only for clearing away plates and refilling water glasses.

2. _T_ The terms "station chef," "line cooks," and "chefs de parties" all mean the same thing.

3. _F_ Paul Bocuse and Pierre Troisgros were very much against the idea of nouvelle cuisine.

4. _T_ There have been many changes in the structure of the "typical" family in this country. These changes have had a direct influence on the foodservice industry.

5. _T_ An increased awareness of nutrition, health, and fitness has helped to make dishes low in fat, cholesterol, and sodium popular.

6. __F__ Aquaculture is a way to force oysters to produce pearls.
7. __T__ A trend and a fad are exactly the same.

Fill in the Blank

1. An agronomist is a person who studies _Food Exploration_
2. An ingredient or dish that is native to a particular area or country is _____. For example, red beans and rice are _____ to New Orleans.
3. A code that explains the proper way to behave in different circumstances is _____.
4. The system of government practiced during the Middle Ages was known as _MONARCHY_____.
5. _haute Cuisine_ is a style of cooking and foods prepared by home cooks for the middle class.
6. A style of cooking and foods prepared by chefs for the upper class in restaurants and hotels and for the wealthy are referred to as _____.
7. The technique used to kill bacteria in foods (especially milk) with heat is called _PASTERIZATION_.
8. A food preservation technique, known as _____, has been used to give perishable items relatively long shelf life, even without refrigeration.
9. The system known as _Hydroponic_ allows foods to be raised without soil. Roots are bathed in a nutrient-rich waterbath instead.
10. "_Chef de Cuisine_" is the French term for "cook."

Discussion

1. *The Epicurean* was written by the first internationally known chef of an American restaurant. Name the chef and the restaurant.
2. Describe the duties of a sous-chef.
3. Describe the duties of the fish station. If there is no separate fish station, who would most likely be responsible for these duties?
4. Name the key positions for the dining room, also known as the "front of the house." Where possible, give both the English and the French terms.
5. Describe the duties of the pantry. What is another name for this station?
6. What are some careers in this industry that do not fit the "standard" picture of chef in a kitchen or dining room manager?
7. How might the traditional brigade system be modified so that it can work with a small number of people in the kitchen?
8. Describe some of the changes in our world today that have had an effect on how food is prepared and served in contemporary restaurants.
9. Who is Caterina de Medici? Why is she important to the history of the foodservice industry?
10. List a few contributions made by Escoffier.

What Went Wrong?

The kitchen is very busy. It is a Saturday night and the dining room is crowded with customers. Everyone is waiting a long time for his or her food. When an unhappy guest gets up to complain, he looks in the kitchen and sees that everyone is running around, and that no one seems to know who is doing what.

They should have some kind of a system such as the Brigade System were everyone is committed to certain positions in the kitchen

Chapter 2

The Professional Chef

This chapter takes a brief look at the chef as a professional. The term "chef" ought to be one of respect. When it is earned through experience, training, and dedication, it *is* a title of respect. Each person will follow a special path to reach his or her ultimate goal. As we saw in the previous chapter, there are many different jobs open in the foodservice industry for people who are willing to take the time and effort to learn through school work, experience, or (ideally) both.

After reading and studying this chapter, you should be able to:

1. Name many of the different characteristics of a true professional.
2. Explain the purpose, tradition, and history of the chef's uniform, especially the hat worn by chefs.
3. Name and explain some fundamental principles used to purchase foods properly.
4. Name and explain some basic procedure for controlling costs.
5. Explain the concept of total utilization.
6. Name some strategies for menu pricing.
7. Describe a number of ways that a restaurant can maintain good relations with its customers.

Matching

1. _____ EP
2. _____ Total utilization
3. _____ Toque blanche
4. _____ AP
5. _____ Purchasing specifications
6. _____ Pleats on a chef's hat
7. _____ Parstock
8. _____ Follow the leader
9. _____ Copy
10. _____ Market quotes

a. Price of foods when they are delivered, before any trimming, cutting, or portioning is done.

b. The chef's tall white hat.

c. Said to represent the number of ways a chef can prepare eggs.

d. Price of foods after all of the inedible trim has been removed.

e. Wasting as little as possible.

f. A written statement of the grade, size, quality, and other pertinent information about the foods being purchased.

g. The current price of goods

h. A menu-pricing strategy; prices are selected to be similar to restaurants like your own.

i. The amount of food necessary to have on hand so that all menu items can be prepared.

j. The words on a menu, including both the name of the item and any written description of them.

Multiple Choice

1. A purchase specification should tell the purveyor
   a. the size of the can or box desired.
   b. the quality grade of meat, poultry, dairy, and produce that receives a quality grade.
   c. the weight of a cut of meat.
   d. the number of apples in a box.
   e. all of the above.
2. A chef needs to know
   a. only how to cook; others are responsible for making a profit.
   b. enough about all aspects of running a business to be certain that the restaurant is able to make a profit.
   c. how to read a French menu.
   d. the names of all the sauces.
3. The first step that must be taken before a chef can start to order foods is to
   a. find the names and telephone numbers of the purveyors in the area.
   b. develop a menu.
   c. build shelves for storage and make necessary repairs to all coolers and freezers.
   d. get a scale to weigh incoming orders.
4. An important reason to wear the chef's uniform is that
   a. it will keep your other clothes from being ruined.
   b. it is instantly recognizable and helps to promote the image of professionalism.
   c. you will blend into the rest of the kitchen without being mistaken for a customer or a salesperson.
   d. it is comfortable.

True/False

1. _____ The chef's jacket is designed for both men and women.

2. _____ A sense of judgment will be mastered once formal education is completed.

3. _____ The chef should never need to hire professionals for assistance with budgeting, taxes, or other business matters if he has been properly trained.

4. _____ An item is priced according to its quality and yield grades, size, and brand.

5. _____ The language used in a kitchen is often a little more "graphic" than in other places, but it is all right, since most kitchen staff members don't mind.

6. _____ A computer can help with purchasing, inventory, billing, costing, and recipe formatting and standardization.

7. _____ The price of the item when it is delivered to the kitchen is known as the EP, or "eventual price."

Fill in the Blank

1. A chef should remember that there is a continual need to grow as a professional. Two ways that this can be done are to _____ and to _____.
2. The customer must always _____.
3. _____ is the primary purpose of being in business.
4. There is a story about the origins of the chef's hat that tells how some chefs to royalty tried to avoid their enemies by _____.
5. When you are trying to find out which purveyors are the most reliable, you can ask the _____ or _____.
6. _____ pricing means that you will make your selling price similar to that of other restaurants.

Discussion

1. Sometimes we are not aware of the ways in which our actions and language can affect others around us. Name some unacceptable behaviors that should never be a part of kitchen etiquette.
2. What are some of the ways that a chef can maintain awareness of the trends in restaurants and develop a good network?
3. Why is judgment so important?
4. Describe the parts of a chef's uniform, and give a history of the chef's hat.
5. Discuss the importance of computers in the contemporary kitchen.

What Went Wrong?

Point out several problems with the restaurant operation in the following situation.

Two couples are leaving a restaurant where they have had dinner. They are discussing their evening. The women agree that they did not feel completely comfortable in the dining room, but they cannot explain exactly why. Both couples wonder why they felt they were eating so quickly. One of the men says that the music was too loud and a little too modern for his taste. None of them wanted to linger after dinner for coffee.

Chapter 3

Sanitation and Safety

Keeping the work environment clean and safe is of primary importance in the foodservice industry. Any shortcomings in these areas could affect the workers and the customers equally. One of the major lessons of this chapter is the prevention of food-borne illness.

After reading and studying this chapter, you should be able to:

1. Understand and explain the importance of keeping the workplace sanitary and safe.
2. Explain proper ways to handle foods and tools so that cross-contamination is eliminated.
3. Describe the importance of keeping foods within the safety zone and explain how temperatures can contribute to the spread of food-borne illness.
4. State what the safety zone is.
5. Identify different types of pathogens and explain how they can make us ill.
6. Explain the difference between a food-borne illness and an intoxication.
7. Identify a number of qualities that might make a food "potentially hazardous," and describe correct handling and storage procedures for these foods.
8. Name three sources of contamination in foods.

Matching

1. _____ Biological contaminants

   a. The use of moist heat or chemicals to kill pathogens.

2. _____ Infection

   b. First in, first out.

3. _____ Preserving

   c. A temperature range from 45°F to 140°F. Certain bacteria tend to reproduce most quickly at this temperature.

4. _____ Fungi

   d. An illness brought on by eating foods containing living pathogens (usually bacteria) that continue to grow in the intestines.

5. _____ Lag phase

   e. Foods that have available moisture and protein and an appropriate pH.

6. _____ Virus

   f. Disease-causing microorganisms known as pathogens.

7. _____ Danger zone

   g. The stage during which bacteria become used to a new environment, so that growth is relatively slow.

8. _____ Sanitizing

   h. Pathogens that reproduce by "reprogramming" a cell to make more virus.

9. _____ FIFO

   i. Any of several methods to prevent contamination and spoilage of foods.

10. _____ Potentially hazardous foods

   j. A group of pathogens that includes molds and yeast.

Multiple Choice

1. A parasite is
   a. a pathogen.
   b. found in another organism known as a "host."
   c. a worm or amoeba, for example.
   d. all of the above.
2. Organisms that are classified according to their oxygen requirements may be
   a. anaerobic or aerobic.
   b. thermophilic or mesophilic.
   c. capable of producing endospores.
3. Adulterated foods
   a. have an immediately recognizable "off" odor.
   b. may be made safe for consumption if they are brought to a boil.
   c. may smell and appear perfectly safe to eat.
   d. will look rotten.
4. To reduce the chance of bacterial contamination of foods, be sure that they are
   a. brought through the danger zone rapidly and then properly stored, labeled, and dated.
   b. taken directly from the stove to the refrigerator to cool quickly.
   c. brought back to a safe temperature as quickly as possible before service.
   d. cooled in plastic because plastic allows food to cool more quickly than other materials.
   e. a and c.
   f. b and d.
5. To prevent cross contamination, remember to
   a. store foods wherever they fit.
   b. clean and sanitize tools during preparation, when switching from one task to another.
   c. use sanitizing solutions, just at the end of each shift.
   d. cut raw foods first, before going on to cut cooked ones.

True/False

1. _____ The control of both time and temperature is an important weapon against pathogens.

2. _____ A pH value of less than 7 indicates an acid food.

3. _____ An example of a food-borne illness caused by a type of virus is salmonellosis.

4. _____ It is not possible to effectively sanitize tools and equipment in a three-compartment sink.

5. _____ Rats, roaches, and flies are unsightly, but they rarely cause illness.

6. _____ Salt or cornmeal will help to absorb grease that has been spilled.

7. _____ There is a time limit of about 2 hours for how long food can be safely held in the danger zone.

8. _____ Foods may be safely thawed by leaving them in plastic tubs in a sink overnight.

9. _____ The decline phase of bacterial growth is when the supplies necessary for life are exhausted and more bacteria are dying than are growing.

10. _____ Negative publicity is one of the ways in which carelessness about sanitation and personal cleanliness can harm a restaurant's business.

Fill in the Blank

1. _____, _____, and _____ are three symptoms of most food-borne illnesses.
2. Physical contaminants are items, such as _____, that fall into food during preparation.
3. The _____ is used to help someone who is choking.
4. _____ occurs when a person eats the toxins produced by a pathogen as it goes through its life cycle.
5. When a food-borne outbreak is declared "official," it involves _____ and has been confirmed by _____.
6. Bacteria reproduce asexually by a means known as _____.

Discussion

1. Name several different points to keep in mind about storing foods safely.
2. What areas should be checked for safety in the kitchen?
3. Describe a typical scene of cross contamination, or give several examples.
4. What is the importance of the spore-forming ability of some bacteria?

What Went Wrong?

A busload of senior citizens on a tour of a wine-growing region stops at a roadside diner. The special of the day was an egg salad platter with coleslaw and potato salad. Several of the tourists ordered it. Several hours later, some began to complain of various symptoms. Eventually, two men and a woman were hospitalized.

Chapter *4*

Nutrition and Nutritional Cooking

Nearly everyone is aware of nutrition. Newspapers and magazines have stories about the increasing amount of links that are being uncovered about the way that the foods we eat can affect our health. Chefs need to learn about nutrition so that they can incorporate some change into their menus, to appeal to the increasing number of customers who would like to have healthy food.

This chapter looks at the basics of nutrition and then discusses the ways that a chef might cook, with nutrition as a goal. After reading and studying this chapter, you should be able to:

1. Name the six basic nutrients and discuss their individual importance.
2. Understand and discuss some of the ways that our diets can affect our health.
3. Describe the various types of fats and oils and explain what is meant by saturated, monounsaturated, and polyunsaturated fats.
4. Explain where cholesterol in the diet is found and what cholesterol's relationship with saturated fats is.
5. Understand and explain how fats in our diets, especially saturated fats, can affect our serum cholesterol levels.
6. Name and discuss the seven dietary guidelines prepared by the U.S. Department of Health and Human Services and the Department of Agriculture.
7. Understand what is meant by RDA levels and how to meet these needs with a varied diet.
8. Describe several practices that can make it possible to serve foods that meet the dietary guidelines when purchasing, preparing, and serving foods.

Matching

1. _____ Polyunsaturated
2. _____ RDA
3. _____ Nutrients
4. _____ Metabolism
5. _____ Amino acid
6. _____ Fiber

a. The structural framework of plants.

b. A calorie that provides only energy in the form of heat.

c. The part of the protein that carries nitrogen.

d. A fatty acid that has two open spaces for hydrogen.

e. A fat-related compound known as a sterol; found only in animal foods.

f. The Recommended Dietary Allowance of various nutrients (protein, vitamins, and minerals), adjusted for age and gender.

7. _____ Empty calorie

g. The sum of the physical and chemical processes necessary to maintain life.

8. _____ Anemia

h. A fatty acid that contains all the hydrogen it can hold.

9. _____ Saturated

i. A deficiency disease brought on by a lack of iron.

10. _____ Cholesterol

j. The components found in foods that the body needs in order to support life.

Multiple Choice

1. The factor(s) most likely to affect cholesterol levels in the blood are
   a. a diet that contains too many high-sodium foods and egg yolks.
   b. excessive drinking and a lack of fiber in diet.
   c. a diet that is high in fats of all sorts, especially saturated fat, combined with smoking and lack of exercise.
   d. the area of the world in which you live and the type of job you have.
2. There are six basic nutrients. Our diets should derive the majority of their calories (55 to 60%) from
   a. fruits, vegetables, whole grains, and dried legumes.
   b. lean meats, skinless breast of chicken, and fish.
   c. eggs, cheese, peanut butter, and mayonnaise.
   d. white bread, jelly, and processed foods.
3. Soluble fiber is found in
   a. oat bran.
   b. rice.
   c. vegetables.
   d. all of the above.
4. Minerals have
   a. no calories.
   b. no taste.
   c. no RDAs.
   d. all of the above.
5. There are no RDAs for carbohydrates and fats because
   a. everyone eats enough of these foods.
   b. everyone has the same need for these nutrients.
   c. individual needs will vary because of differences in age, weight, gender, activity level, and stress.
   d. people should be encouraged to stop eating foods that contain these nutrients.
6. To make nutritional cooking more effective, the chef can
   a. learn to purchase low- or nonfat ingredients wherever possible.
   b. cut back on the portion size for protein-rich foods.
   c. eliminate butter, cream, and bacon from the kitchen.
   d. a and c.
   e. a and b.

True/False

1. _____ Fats and oils are classified according to the amount of nitrogen in their structure.

2. _____ Most oils derived from nuts and seeds are highly saturated.

3. _____ Cholesterol is found only in foods that come from animals.

4. _____ There are eight essential amino acids that we must consume every day.

5. _____ There are two types of fiber: soluble and insoluble.

6. _____ The body is capable of digesting fiber.

7. _____ Vitamins and minerals provide important nutrients to the body, but they do not contain any calories.

8. _____ Water is the most frequently forgotten nutrient that our bodies need to maintain health.

9. _____ The best way to retain nutrients in vegetables of all types is to cook them slowly.

10. _____ Sauces should almost always be eliminated in a dish that is supposed to be nutritional.

11. _____ Grilling, roasting, and steaming are all good techniques for nutritional cooking, since they do not require the addition of fats and oils.

Fill in the Blank

1. _____ is the body's preferred source of fuel.
2. Most oils derived from plants are either polyunsaturated or monounsaturated. _____ and _____ are two exceptions to this general statement.
3. The mineral closely linked with healthy bones and teeth is _____.
4. _____ is a cooking technique that gives a special smoky taste to roasted foods, without requiring brines or cures.
5. A person's diet should include _____, to be sure that all 50 of the known nutrients are represented in the diet.
6. A safe weight loss program would rely upon _____ and _____.

Discussion

1. What might be the consequences of a fad diet that allows only one food to be eaten?
2. What are the general characteristics of most saturated fats?
3. There are 22 amino acids that the body needs, yet we are asked to include only eight of them in our diets. Why?
4. What are the factors that affect blood cholesterol levels?
5. What is the basic difference between the typical American diet and that suggested as a goal by the Senate Select Committee on Nutrition?
6. How can the four basic food groups act as a menu planner?
7. What are some of the ways that careful purchasing can help with nutritional cooking?
8. What are additives? Are they all bad for us?
9. How can cooking and presentation techniques affect the success or failure of nutritional cooking?

What Went Wrong?

The menu has an entrée selection that sounds appealing and healthy. A customer orders it, but is unhappy with what he receives. He feels he has not been given enough food for the money he has paid.

Chapter 5

Equipment
Identification

One of the signs of a true professional is the ability to use tools properly and carefully, so that tasks in the kitchen can be performed efficiently. This means that the chef must be able to identify tools and select the right piece of equipment for the job. It is also crucial that large equipment be used correctly, the same way it is important to handle small tools with care.

After reading and studying this chapter, you should be able to:

1. Recognize a variety of different knives, small tools, and hand-operated equipment, and be able to use them properly.
2. Hone and sharpen most knives, using a steel and a sharpening stone.
3. Name several tools used to measure ingredients and temperatures.
4. Recognize the different pans used for cooking on top of the stove and in the oven.
5. Describe the advantages and disadvantages of the different materials used to produce pots and pans.
6. Recognize, assemble, operate, and clean larger equipment, including slicers, choppers, mixers, and blenders.
7. Name several different refrigerated storage units, including walk-ins, reach-ins, and on-site refrigeration.
8. Name, operate, and clean a variety of steam-jacketed kettles, steamers, and ovens.

Matching

1. _____ Gratin dish
2. _____ Rondeau
3. _____ Rat-tail tang
4. _____ Steel
5. _____ Spider
6. _____ Drum sieve
7. _____ Marmite
8. _____ Timbale mold
9. _____ Buffalo chopper
10. _____ Mandolin

a. A hand-held tool used to lift foods out of the cooking liquid or oil.

b. A stove-top pot that is wider than it is deep.

c. A stock pot.

d. A hand-operated slicing device.

e. A large piece of equipment used to mince, chop, or grind foods.

f. An oven-proof oval dish used to prepare and serve foods that are cooked under a broiler or salamander.

g. The tool used to hone knives.

h. The type of tang in which only a thin rod of metal attaches the blade to the handle of a knife.

i. A small earthenware or metal mold used to prepare individual portions of molded cooked foods.

j. A type of sieve in which a wire mesh is clamped in a circular hoop.

13

Multiple Choice

1. A good chef's knife should be
   a. made in Germany or Switzerland.
   b. made of carbon steel.
   c. no more than 8 inches long.
   d. made with a full tang and a tapered blade.
2. A chinois is used to
   a. strain soups, sauces, and batters.
   b. purée foods.
   c. fold one ingredient into another.
   d. stir foods in a wok.
3. It is a good idea to hone a knife on a steel
   a. once or twice a week.
   b. several times while working with the knife.
   c. only after using sharpening stones.
   d. never, because it might dull the knife.
4. All types of knives should always have
   a. taper ground blades.
   b. rat-tail tangs.
   c. a bolster.
   d. not necessarily any of the above, because it depends upon the actual type of knife.
5. Another name for a chef's knife is
   a. French knife.
   b. pizza cutter.
   c. master knife.
   d. all-purpose knife.

True/False

1. _____ The metal fasteners used to hold the knife together are known as rivets.
2. _____ Anodized aluminum and stainless steel are generally not used for making stock pots.
3. _____ A bain-marie is used to panfry foods over high heat.
4. _____ A food processor is capable of performing many different functions, including slicing, grinding, pureeing, and grating.
5. _____ A ring-top range has openings that can be made larger and smaller by removing additional rings. This is the way that the temperature is controlled.
6. _____ A walk-in cooler is larger than other types of refrigerators; some are large enough to accommodate rolling carts for additional storage.
7. _____ A convection steamer does not build up pressure in the cooking chamber, so it can be opened without venting the chamber first.
8. _____ A convection oven relies upon infrared lights to help cook foods quickly.
9. _____ Microwave ovens are not suitable for use in commercial kitchens.
10. _____ A food mill is used to grind whole grains for use in breads and cereals.

Fill in the Blank

1. _____ and _____ can be used to make certain that the right size portion is served to each customer.
2. A triple-faced sharpening stone, with three surfaces mounted on a wheel, is often known as an _____.
3. A small knife, shaped like a bird's beak, that is used to cut vegetables and flute mushrooms is a _____.
4. A blade made by combining two sheets of metal and beveling their edges is a _____.
5. A French term for the collection of knives and tools that a chef will assemble throughout a career is _____.
6. Three of the small tools (not knives) often found in a cook's or chef's knife kit might be _____, _____, and _____.
7. The three different types of thermometers frequently used in the kitchen are _____, _____, and _____.
8. Pots made of _____ are usually quick to respond to changes in heat, require extensive upkeep, and are the most expensive type to buy.

Discussion

1. Why is the chef's knife so important, and why is it a good idea to buy the best knife you can find?
2. Describe some of the places that refrigerated storage would be good to have in a kitchen.
3. Describe the procedure for honing and sharpening a knife.
4. What are the benefits of deck ovens, rotary ovens, pizza ovens, and convection ovens?
5. What are the benefits and disadvantages of copper cookware?
6. Describe the basic parts of a chef's knife and what each part has to do with the way the knife performs.
7. What types of equipment are important to have available for measuring?
8. Why are sieves, strainers, cheesecloths, blenders, and food processors important in the kitchen?

What Went Wrong?

Most of the time, injuries in the kitchen are the result of carelessness while operating and cleaning equipment. When the prep cook began to clean the slicer, something went wrong and he was badly injured.

Chapter 6

Meats, Poultry, and Game Identification

This chapter discusses the basic methods of raising, slaughtering, and butchering a variety of meats, as well as quality and inspection standards. After reading and studying this chapter, you should be able to:

1. Handle and store meats properly after they are received.
2. Understand the inspection and grading (quality and yield) standards used by the U.S. Department of Agriculture.
3. Draw correlations between the basic carcass divisions of large animals (beef, veal, pork, lamb, and large game).
4. Identify a number of market forms for each type of meat (beef, veal, pork, lamb, and large game).
5. Understand the classification and grades applied to a variety of birds, including domestic poultry and game birds.
6. Identify a variety of birds, including domestic poultry and game birds.
7. Identify offal meats (also known as variety meats).
8. Define and understand what is meant by "kosher meats."

Matching

1. _____ Yield grade

    a. A term used to describe beef that is eventually cut into the rib, the chuck, the brisket, and the foreshank.

2. _____ "PC"

    b. A special type of air-tight, plastic wrapping, used for storing all types of meats and poultry.

3. _____ Aging

    c. A term used to describe sheep slaughtered after one year of age.

4. _____ Primal cut

    d. These cuts of meat are considered the "innards" of any animal.

5. _____ Offal

    e. A term used to describe prefabricated meat cut into portions.

6. _____ Forequarter

    f. The portions produced by the initial cutting of an animal carcass.

7. _____ Mutton

    g. A term used to describe beef that is eventually cut into the loin and the leg.

8. _____ Free-range

    h. A term used for farm-raised venison (deer).

9. _____ Cryovac

i. These are meats that are specially slaughtered, bled, and fabricated in order to comply with religious dietary laws.

10. _____ Hindquarter

j. A term used for sheep slaughtered under one year of age.

11. _____ Kosher meats

k. A process that gives beef a darker color, a more tender texture, and a full flavor.

12. _____ Fallow deer

l. A grade given to beef that reflects the yield of usable meat versus fat trim.

13. _____ Lamb

m. A term used to describe poultry that is raised in large yards.

Multiple Choice

1. Because lamb is slaughtered when still quite young, it is tender, and most cuts can be cooked by
   a. any method.
   b. broiling and grilling.
   c. sautéing and panfrying.
   d. stewing and braising.
   e. deep-frying.
2. The fattened livers of a special type of goose or duck are called
   a. sweetbreads.
   b. foie gras.
   c. tripe.
   d. teal.
   e. none of the above.
3. Poultry is given a mandatory inspection for wholesomeness and may be graded as
   a. USDA 1, 2, or 3.
   b. Prime, Choice, Good, or Utility.
   c. USDA A, B, or C.
   d. Prime, Choice, Select, Standard, Commercial, Utility, Cutter, and Canner.
   e. none of the above
4. A capon is another name for a
   a. fryer.
   b. guinea hen.
   c. stewing hen.
   d. castrated male chicken.
   e. squab.
5. Cuts of veal are similar to those of
   a. lamb.
   b. beef.
   c. mutton.
   d. pork.
   e. none of the above.

True/False

1. _____ Grading of meats by the USDA is not mandatory.

2. _____ Sweetbreads are the thymus gland of veal or lamb.

3. _____ Fallow deer produces a lean, tasty meat with less fat and cholesterol than beef.

4. _____ Veal is an offshoot of the beef industry.

5. _____ A Yield 1 grade in beef would reflect the lowest amount of usable meat versus fat trim.

Fill in the Blank

1. Offal meats are divided into two categories: _____ and _____.
2. Poultry are _____; that is, their habitat and breeding are carefully controlled by humans.
3. Sheep slaughtered under a year of age may still be labeled _____; if slaughtered after that, however, they must be labeled _____.
4. Government inspection of all meats is _____.
5. Aged beef is more expensive because a significant _____ and _____ loss reduces ultimate _____.

Discussion

1. What determines the types of meat cuts an establishment will buy? Explain your answer.
2. Briefly describe the proper procedure for storing meats.
3. What is Cryovac?
4. At what point is meat inspected by the USDA?
5. What are the USDA regulations on grading meats?
6. What are the eight grades of beef?
7. What are the five grades of veal?
8. What will determine the grade of any given animal?
9. What are the three grades of poultry?
10. What factors are judged when grading poultry?
11. List and describe the four general carcass divisions.
12. What is a primal cut?
13. What will determine the price of a cut of meat in relation to its fabrication?
14. What types of meats are assigned quality grades?
15. What is a yield grade and how is it determined?
16. What primal cuts are in a forequarter of beef?
17. What primal cuts are in a hindquarter of beef?
18. What is the process of aging beef? What happens to the ultimate yield of aged beef?
19. At what age are veal slaughtered?
20. What are the primal cuts of veal?
21. What other parts of veal are highly prized?
22. What are the primal cuts of pork?
23. What is the difference between lamb and mutton?
24. Why are spring and hot-house lamb not grass-fed?
25. What are the primal cuts of lamb?
26. What is a fallow deer?
27. How does venison compare in fat and cholesterol to beef?
28. How is rabbit raised, and what is its availability?
29. How are the different parts of a rabbit prepared?
30. What are free-range chickens, and how are they raised?
31. How are poultry classified?
32. What is the difference between game birds and domesticated poultry?
33. What are offal meats, and why are they becoming more popular on contemporary menus?
34. How are offal meats categorized? Give as many examples of each as possible.
35. What are kosher meats, and why are they different than other non-kosher meats?
36. Why is the hindquarter of beef not used for kosher meats?
37. As consumers eat smaller portions of meats, what qualities must these meats possess?
38. What guidelines should be observed if the quest is to perceive a meal as healthy and of good value?

What Went Wrong?

1. Even though the rump roast of venison has a good flavor, it is tough and hard to chew. It seems dry, also.
2. A guest complains that an entrée, poached supreme of chicken, is tough.

Chapter 7

Fish and Shellfish Identification

This chapter introduces a variety of fish and shellfish to the student, and categorizes them according to type (flat, round, univalve, bivalve, crustacean, and cephalopod). After reading and studying this chapter, you should be able to:

1. Apply the appropriate standards and tests for quality and freshness.
2. Properly store fish after it is received in the kitchen.
3. Identify the basic market forms of fish.
4. Identify a variety of round fish, flat fish, nonbony fish, univalves, bivalves, crustaceans, and cephalopods, as well as some miscellaneous items (caviar, frog's legs).

Matching

1. _____ Whole or round fish

    a. These fish have a backbone that runs through the center of the fish with four fillets, two upper and two lower.

2. _____ Univalve

    b. A cross-section cut of fish with a portion of the backbone in each cut.

3. _____ Fillet

    c. Shellfish with jointed exterior skeletons or shells.

4. _____ Crustaceans

    d. Single-shelled shellfish.

5. _____ Dressed fish

    e. Fish that is sold exactly as it is caught, completely intact.

6. _____ Nonbony fish

    f. These fish have a backbone, with two fillets on either side.

7. _____ Round fish

    g. A term translated as "head-footed," a reflection of the fact that the tentacles and arms are attached directly to the head.

8. _____ Drawn fish

    h. A boneless piece of fish removed from either side of the backbone.

9. _____ Steaks

    i. Fish that have cartilage instead of bones; ray, skate, sharks, or monkfish.

10. _____ Flat fish

    j. The term used to describe shellfish that have two shells joined by a hinge.

11. _____ Caviar

12. _____ Cephalopods

13. _____ Bivalve

k. Fish sold that have the viscera, scales, and fins removed. The head and tail may also be removed, depending on the fish.

l. A fish that is sold with the viscera removed, but with the head, tail, and fins still intact.

m. A term used to describe the salted roe of the sturgeon fish.

Multiple Choice

1. Very lean fish, such as flounder or sole, are most successfully prepared by
   a. grilling or broiling.
   b. braising or stewing.
   c. poêléing.
   d. poaching or sautéing.
   e. all of the above.
2. The term used to describe the result of improper packaging or thawing and refreezing of frozen seafood is called
   a. belly burn.
   b. freezer burn.
   c. planking.
   d. baccala.
   e. none of the above.
3. If hardshell clams are more than three inches in diameter, they generally are referred to as
   a. little necks.
   b. littlenecks.
   c. quahogs.
   d. cherrystones.
   e. any of the above.
4. The tomalley of a lobster is actually the
   a. liver.
   b. stomach.
   c. brains.
   d. pancreas or thymus.
   e. none of the above.
5. The best way to pair a fish with a cooking technique is to consider
   a. where it was caught.
   b. its flesh.
   c. what the fish naturally feeds on in the wild.
   d. whether or not it is a round fish, flat fish, or a nonbony fish.
   e. none of the above.

True/False

1. _____ Crabs, lobsters, and other live shellfish can be stored in their original shipping containers until they are ready to be prepared.
2. _____ One of the only true soles is the lemon sole.
3. _____ Shrimp are sold according to the number in a pound, known as the "count."

4. _____ Clams, mussels, and oysters should be stored in the bag in which they were delivered, but should not be iced.

5. _____ A whelk is a univalve that comes from the Caribbean and is most accurately classified as a gastropod—a large class of mollusc.

Fill in the Blank

1. _____ occurs when the _____ are not removed promptly from fish; the stomach enzymes begin to eat the flesh, causing it to come away from the bones.
2. _____ is the removal of a mollusc or fish from the shell; this term also refers to its market form, which is sold as meat only, along with natural juices known as _____.
3. Clams and oysters that are sold live in the shell are generally marketed by the _____ from which they were harvested.
4. From the spring through the summer, when the crab molts, blue crab are sold as _____.
5. Real caviar is the _____ from the _____.

Discussion

1. What should be checked when evaluating fresh shellfish?
2. When fish arrives in an establishment, what four steps should be followed?
3. Why is flaked or shaved ice preferred when storing fresh fish?
4. How often should fresh fish be drained and re-iced?
5. How should clams, mussels, and oysters be stored?
6. What is the best way to store shucked scallops?
7. What is the best way to store live crabs, lobsters, or other shellfish?
8. What is the best way to store frozen fish?
9. What is "freezer burn," and how can it be avoided?
10. Briefly describe the following market forms of fish and shellfish:
    a. Whole or round fish.
    b. Drawn fish.
    c. Dressed fish.
    d. Steaks.
    e. Fillets.
    f. Shucked.
11. Briefly describe the following categories of fish and shellfish:
    a. Round fish.
    b. Flat fish.
    c. Nonbony fish.
    d. Univalves.
    e. Bivalves.
    f. Crustaceans.
    g. Cephalopods.
12. What is the difference between the market-form round fish and the category of round fish?
13. What is the difference between true conch and a whelk?
14. Name three examples of nonbony fish.
15. Briefly describe the following types of clams:
    a. Bean clam, or "coquina."
    b. Hardshell clam, or quahog.
    c. Little neck.
    d. Littleneck.
    e. Cherrystone.
    f. Softshell clams.

16. How are clams and oysters generally marketed?
17. List and briefly describe the three species of scallops of commercial importance.
18. What are Coquilles Saint-Jacques?
19. List and briefly describe the different types of Atlantic and Pacific crab.
20. What is the difference between a crayfish and a lobster?
21. How do you determine the sex of a lobster?
22. What does a shrimp "count" mean?

What Went Wrong?

1. The fish that were delivered yesterday now smell rotten, despite the fact that they were immediately iced down.
2. The guest returned the poached bluefish, saying that it had a unpleasant flavor and texture. The fish was very fresh and of high quality when the chef checked it immediately before cooking.

Chapter 8

Fruit, Vegetable, and Fresh Herb Identification

This chapter introduces a wide variety of considerations for the chef who will be purchasing fresh produce. Quality standards, seasonal availability, and storage practices are included. After reading and studying this chapter, you should be able to:

1. Apply general guidelines for selecting the highest quality produce.
2. Store fresh produce properly and retain quality and preserve flavor, color, and nutrients.
3. Identify a variety of fruits, vegetables, and fresh herbs.

Matching

1. _____ Mushrooms

2. _____ Gourd family

3. _____ Hydroponics

4. _____ Roots

5. _____ Herbs

6. _____ Summer squash

7. _____ Tubers

8. _____ Cabbage family

9. _____ Winter squash

a. A vegetable that is a nutrient reservoir for the plant; this category includes radishes, beets, and parsnips.

b. Members of the gourd family that are characterized by their hard rind and seeds.

c. The leaves of aromatic plants used primarily to add flavor to foods.

d. Vegetables that are grown in nutrient-rich water, instead of soil.

e. An enlarged bulbous root capable of generating a new plant; included in this category are potatoes, yams, and sweet potatoes.

f. A family of vegetables that includes kale, turnips, and rutabagas.

g. Cucumbers, eggplant, and many squash varieties are members of this family.

h. A type of edible fungus that is available in cultivated and wild varieties.

i. Squash that are picked while still immature, to insure delicate flesh, tender seeds, and thin skins.

Multiple Choice

1. Most of the "fire" in hot chili peppers is in the
   a.   skin.
   b.   stalk.
   c.   ribs.
   d.   seeds.
   e.   none of the above.

2. Artichokes, fennel, and asparagus are considered
   a.   part of the cabbage family.
   b.   leafy vegetables.
   c.   shoots and stalks.
   d.   members of the onion family.
   e.   none of the above.

3. Fresh herbs are usually added to a dish
   a.   at the end of the cooking process.
   b.   at the beginning of the cooking process.
   c.   after the cooking process is finished.
   d.   as soon as possible.
   e.   none of the above.

4. A substance that can promote ripening in some unripe fruits, but that can also promote spoilage in fruits and vegetables that are already ripe is called
   a.   oxalic acid.
   b.   fermentation.
   c.   oxidation.
   d.   ethylene gas.
   e.   none of the above.

5. Grapes are fruits that are technically
   a.   cherries.
   b.   berries.
   c.   plums.
   d.   tubers.
   e.   none of the above.

True/False

1. _____ All peaches fall into two categories—clingstone and freestone.

2. _____ All peppers start out green and ripen after they are picked.

3. _____ White varieties of grapefruit are generally sweeter than pink varieties.

4. _____ Apples and pears are harvested while still slightly immature and allowed to mature off the tree.

5. _____ Hydroponically grown vegetables may have a less pronounced flavor than conventionally grown fruits or vegetables.

Fill in the Blank

1. Apples and pears are divided into two groups: _____, which last only a short season, and _____, which store well for longer periods of time.

2. Oranges come in three basic varieties: _____, _____, and _____.

3. Cooking plums are generally _____ and _____ than _____ plums.

4. The four major types of melons are: _____, _____, _____, and _____.

5. Once picked, pod and seed vegetables convert their _____ into _____.

Discussion

1. When will most produce have a noticeably better quality and flavor?
2. What are the advantages of buying fruit and produce from local or "boutique" purveyors?
3. What is hydroponics? What is one advantage and one disadvantage of hydroponically grown vegetables and fruit?
4. What is the best temperature and humidity to store fruits and vegetables? What are some exceptions to these guidelines?
5. Why should most fruits be kept dry?
6. At what temperature should fruits and vegetables be stored if they need to be ripened?
7. What are some fruits that give off odors and what are some that can absorb odors?
8. Briefly explain the two groups of apples and pears.
9. What should be taken into consideration when purchasing berries?
10. What are the three varieties of oranges?
11. What are the four major types of melons?
12. What are the two categories of peaches? Explain each category.
13. What part of the rhubarb plant can be eaten?
14. What can be said about the ripening process with tropical fruits?
15. Turnips and rutabagas are members of what vegetable family?
16. What is the difference between winter and summer squashes?
17. What are some of the available forms of mushrooms?
18. How are bell peppers ripened?
19. Where is most of the "fire" in hot chili peppers?
20. Why are pod and seed vegetables best eaten when young and fresh?
21. Why are some pod vegetables eaten without their pods?
22. What is the difference between a root vegetable and a tuber?
23. What is the best way to store root vegetables and tubers?
24. What are herbs?
25. What is a good indicator of quality in fresh herbs?
26. What guidelines should be followed for the correct use of fresh herbs?
27. What is the best way to store fresh herbs?
28. What is another advantage of buying fresh fruit and vegetables from local growers?

What Went Wrong?

1. The salsa made with fresh tomatoes is usually so popular that it is difficult to keep the customers supplied fast enough. Ever since summer ended, though, demand for salsa has fallen off.
2. A bunch of bananas was left near a basket of ripe peaches. The next day, the peaches were rotten.

Chapter 9

Dairy, Cheese, and Egg Identification

Most kitchens stock a supply of different types of dairy products, including butter, cream, and milk. Eggs are used throughout the entire kitchen, and cheese often plays a starring role in a recipe. However, these foods are so "ordinary" that some people may take them for granted. But just because they are readily available is no reason to suspend the usual care taken to buy the best possible items.

After reading and studying this chapter, you should be able to:

1. Recognize and describe a variety of milk and milk-based beverages.
2. Describe and use the correct procedures for handling and storing dairy and egg products, to be sure they retain their quality, freshness, and safety.
3. Describe what is meant by pasteurization, and name the three temperature ranges at which it can be done.
4. Name the quality grades assigned to milk and dairy products, and list some of the factors used to determine what quality grade is awarded.
5. Name the different categories used to group natural cheese, list a number of their specific characteristics, and identify a number of cheeses within each of the categories.
6. Identify the various sizes used for eggs, and describe how eggs are graded.

Matching

1. _____ Date stamp

2. _____ Homogenized

3. _____ Granites

4. _____ Natural cheese

5. _____ Sweet butter

6. _____ Gorgonzola

7. _____ Chalazae

8. _____ Pasteurization

9. _____ Skim milk

10. _____ Rennet

a. A frozen dessert produced by freezing a flavored syrup and then scraping to create large grains or crystals.

b. A type of blue-veined cheese made in Italy from cow's or goat's milk.

c. A cheese that is considered "living" because its characteristics will follow a cycle of immaturity, ripeness, and overripeness.

d. Heating an item to a specific temperature for a certain period of time, to destroy various microorganisms.

e. Milk with less than 0.1% butterfat.

f. An enzyme combined with milk to prepare cheese.

g. The date on a carton of milk or cream that indicates the last day it can be sold.

h. The twisted membranes that hold the yolk in place.

i. Butter made from sweet cream.

j. Milk that has been treated so that the butterfat will not separate and rise to the top.

Multiple Choice

1. Examples of semi-soft cheeses are
    a. Roquefort and Danish bleu.
    b. Gouda and Edam.
    c. Parmesan and Sapsago.
    d. Brie and Camembert.
2. A fresh cheese is
    a. usually salty and dry.
    b. strongly flavored.
    c. mild, creamy in texture.
    d. always made from sheep's milk.
3. The egg yolk is capable of
    a. making a foam.
    b. making an emulsion.
    c. making a glaze.
    d. all of the above.
4. The smallest eggs are named
    a. pee wee.
    b. tiny.
    c. small.
    d. bantam.
5. If the label on a package of butter says "Sweet Butter," it may not necessarily mean
    a. that the butter is sweet to the taste.
    b. that the butter is fresh.
    c. that no salt was added to the butter.
6. Pasteurized foods do not
    a. continue to ripen.
    b. spoil.
    c. taste fresh.
    d. have a place in the kitchen.
7. A good quality vanilla ice cream must have a minimum of
    a. 8% butterfat.
    b. 12% egg yolks.
    c. 50% heavy cream.
    d. 10% butterfat.

True/False

1. _____ Cream is always separated from milk by simply allowing it to rise naturally to the surface.

2. _____ The color of butter is the same all year round.

3. _____ Crème fraîche is a sweet, fresh cream.

4. _____ The younger that the hen is laying the eggs, the smaller the egg will be.

5. _____ An egg white contains a significant amount of fat.

6. _____ Hard cheeses, such as cheddar, grate easily.

7. _____ Roquefort cheese is made from raw sheep's milk.

8. _____ Half and half contains as much milkfat as light cream.

9. _____ If milk were pasteurized on June 10, the date stamp should read July 2.

10. _____ Milkfat and butterfat are the same thing.

Fill in the Blank

1. A soft cheese, such as Brie, has a surface mold that causes the cheese to ripen from _____.
2. Buttermilk is traditionally the portion of milk left after churning butter, but today most buttermilk is made by adding _____.
3. When rennet is combined with milk, it causes the milk solids to coagulate into _____.
4. The name of the procedure when milk products are heated to 166°F for 30 seconds is _____.
5. Sherbet is the closest English translation for the French term _____.
6. Low-fat and skim milk is always fortified with _____ and _____.

Discussion

1. Why is low-fat and skim milk fortified with Vitamins A and D?
2. What are the indications that ice cream is not of very good quality?
3. Why are eggs so important in the kitchen?
4. Why do some chefs feel that ultrapasteurized cream is less desirable?
5. Why might a chef prefer unsalted butter?

What Went Wrong?

The milk and cream kept at the waiter's station for coffee and tea is frequently left out during the entire service period. Even though the date stamps say that the milk should be wholesome and safe to serve, it curdles as soon as it is poured into a hot beverage.

Chapter 10

Nonperishable Goods Identification

A well-stocked kitchen has a great variety of foods available so that all the dishes listed on the menu can be prepared. In addition to the foods covered in the first four chapters in this section, there are other items that can be stored for longer periods. These foods are known as dry or nonperishable goods.

After reading and studying this chapter, you should be able to:

1. Identify and name some of the major uses for a variety of grains, meals, and flours.
2. Identify and name some of the traditional uses for dried legumes.
3. Identify a variety of dried pastas and noodles, and name some of the dishes prepared using them.
4. Identify and describe sugars, syrups, and other sweeteners commonly found in the kitchen.
5. Describe briefly the purchase forms of coffee and tea, and how they should be stored.
6. Identify a variety of dry goods used for baking, including chocolate, leaveners, thickeners, extracts, and flavorings.
7. Identify a variety of nuts and seeds, give their common purchase forms, and explain how they are stored.
8. Identify oils and shortenings used in the kitchen, and explain which factors might help determine when and how they are used in cooking and baking.
9. Identify a number of vinegars and condiments.
10. Identify the dried herbs and spices commonly required by the chef, and how they should be stored and used.
11. Identify various forms of salt and pepper, and explain their importance to the chef.
12. Name a number of wines, cordials, and liqueurs used in cooking.
13. Identify various can sizes and the quality factors used to select canned, frozen, and convenience foods.
14. Explain the importance of the FIFO rule, as it relates to nonperishable goods.

Matching

1. _D_ Goober
2. _I_ Treacle
3. _E_ Chocolate liquor
4. _B_ Soba noodles
5. _H_ Miso
6. _A_ Kasha
7. _F_ Fusilli
8. _J_ Pignoli
9. _C_ Rapeseed oil
10. _G_ MSG

a. Buckwheat groats.

b. Buckwheat noodles popular in Japanese cuisine.

c. Oil extracted from seeds of plants related to the turnip.

d. Another term for peanut.

e. A coarse paste made by grinding the nibs of cocoa beans.

f. Twisted, corkscrew-shaped pasta.

g. A flavor enhancer used in Chinese food and in processed foods.

h. A fermented paste made from soybeans.

i. A type of strongly flavored molasses; may be light or dark.

j. Pine nuts.

Multiple Choice

1. Farina is a meal made by grinding
   a. wheat.
   b. corn.
   c. rice.
   d. barley.
2. Dried herbs should not be stored
   a. in glass jars.
   b. in a dark closet.
   c. on a shelf over the stove-top.
   d. in the refrigerator.
3. Coffee may be purchased as
   a. a prepared beverage.
   b. whole beans, instant, or preground.
   c. decaffeinated, dark roast, or medium roast.
   d. b and c.
   e. all of the above.
4. Black-eyed peas are an important ingredient in
   a. jambalaya.
   b. Hoppin' John.
   c. pasta e fagioli.
   d. falafel.
5. Whole grains have not been
   a. refined and polished.
   b. separated from the bran and germ.
   c. threshed and graded.
   d. a and b.
   e. a and c.
6. Salt is usually
   a. mined and refined, and then iodine is added to it.
   b. combined with pepper and used as a seasoning blend.

c. used for a variety of purposes in the kitchen, so there may be a need to have a number of different types of salt available.

d. bad for you.

True/False

1. _T_ There are different types of tofu, sold as firm, silky, or soft.
2. _F_ Couscous is made from cornmeal.
3. _F_ Masa harina is used to make flour tortillas.
4. _T_ There is more than one kind of lentil.
5. _F_ Basmati is a type of cereal.
6. _T_ The bran is the outer covering of a grain. It is often removed during processing and refining.
7. _T_ Dry goods should be in clean, dry packaging when they are received.
8. _F_ Cellophane noodles are made from wheat flour.

Fill in the Blank

1. The cuisine that includes noodles named somen and soba is _Jap_.
2. A dark brown product with a flavor slightly similar to chocolate that is used as a chocolate replacement is known as _CAROB_.
3. The sweetener made by reducing the sap of a tree is known as _MAPLE SYRUP_.
4. A spice used to flavor marinades used with game is _JUNIPER BERRIES_.
5. One of the most prized of all peppercorns is the _TELLICHERY_.
6. A #10 can is the equivalent of _3 ½_ #2½ cans.
7. Lard often undergoes a process called _DEODERIZATION_, to neutralize any odors.

Discussion

1. Why are dried pastas considered a "convenience food"?
2. Name at least ten different flours, grains, or meals, and give their major uses or the name of a specific dish associated with them.
3. What are dried legumes?
4. What happens when a whole grain is milled?
5. Name a number of different sugars and syrups used in the kitchen as sweeteners.
6. Give the melting and smoking point for the following fats and oils:
    a. Clarified butter. 95° 300°
    b. Sunflower oil. 2° 400°
    c. Lard. 92° 375°
    d. Corn oil. 12 450°
7. Describe paprika.

What Went Wrong?

The soup made from black beans was gritty, with a moldy flavor.

Chapter 11

Meat Fabrication

The material included in this chapter is intended as an introduction to various butchering and fabricating techniques that can be applied to most meats. Even if a kitchen is supplied with mainly prefabricated meats, there are a few special skills included here that may be of assistance.

After reading and studying this chapter, you should be able to:

1. Name some of the important basics for fabricating meats of all sorts.
2. Tie a roast of meat, using two different methods.
3. Identify some of the key points of trimming and boning a loin of pork.
4. Briefly describe the way to trim a tenderloin.
5. Describe the steps involved in butterflying meats.
6. Name some of the cuts that can be made from the tenderloin or loin of various meats.
7. Explain the procedure for shaping a medallion and give a few reasons why this step is considered important.
8. Name the steps in cutting and pounding scallops (or cutlets) of meat.
9. Explain what is meant by "frenching" a rack of lamb.
10. Identify some of the steps used when preparing variety meats, such as sweetbreads, liver, kidneys, tongue, and marrow bones.

Matching

1. __G__ Paillard
2. __B__ Frenching
3. __E__ Butterflying
4. __A__ Silverskin
5. __H__ Noisettes

6. _____ Scallop
7. __D__ Chateubriand
8. _____ Grenadin
9. __J__ Sweetbread
10. __C__ Emince

a. The tough membrane covering the tenderloin.

b. Removing all meat and fat, scraping bones clean.

c. The French term for "minced."

d. A cut from the tenderloin of beef.

e. Cutting horizontally through a thick piece of meat to create one that is thinner and has greater surface area.

f. A large, boneless cut from the loin.

g. A pounded cutlet that is frequently grilled.

h. Little "nuts" of meat.

i. Scallopini, escalop, and cutlet are all similar to this cut.

j. A type of variety meat that is blanched before final preparation.

33

Multiple Choice

1. The names used for cuts of meat on the menu are
   a. always different than those used by the purveyor.
   b. are always French.
   c. may not always be used when ordering the meat from the butcher.
   d. are difficult to pronounce.
2. The silverskin should be removed before sautéing or grilling foods because
   a. it can pucker and shrink, causing the meat to cook unevenly.
   b. it tastes bad.
   c. it is not kosher.
   d. it is a sure sign that the kitchen is not doing its job correctly.
3. The proper sequence to follow when preparing sweetbreads is to
   a. peel, press, and then blanch them.
   b. rinse them, blanch in a court bouillon, cool, peel away membrane, and then press.
   c. soak in cold salted water overnight, blanch in hot oil, press, and then peel.
   d. none of the above.
4. A leg of veal can be boned out by
   a. making several parallel cuts down to the bone and peeling away the meat.
   b. pulling out the bone with pliers.
   c. using a band saw to make several cross cuts and then cutting out the pieces of bone from each cut.
   d. using the tip of a boning knife to cut along the natural seams in the meat until the bone is exposed and can be cut away from the meat.

True/False

1. _____ There is more than one way to properly tie a roast.

2. _____ The technique for a tying a roast with the bone in is very different from that used for a boneless roast.

3. _____ The seams found in a large cut of meat, such as a leg of veal or lamb, are the natural separation between individual muscles.

4. _____ Tongue can be tough if it is not handled properly.

5. _____ Butterflying meats is an old-fashioned technique that is never used in a contemporary kitchen.

6. _____ Paillards are always panfried.

7. _____ A scallop is one of many terms used to refer to thin, boneless cuts from the loin, leg, or round.

Fill in the Blank

1. The technique used to increase the surface area of a cutlet and to give it an even thickness is _____.
2. Some names of menu terms for cuts from the tenderloin include _____.
3. The menu term for a cut of meat that is derived from the French term for a straw bed is _____.
4. A medallion or other cut from the loin or tenderloin is wrapped in cheesecloth and gently shaped, in order to _____.
5. The procedure used to cut a rabbit into pieces is called _____.

Discussion

1. Why should a chef be familiar with menu terms as well as the names for cuts used by purveyors?
2. What is the benefit of being able to order larger cuts and fabricate them yourself?

3. What is the marrow?
4. Why might someone worry about ordering a dish of kidneys? How can it be prepared so that the worry is not a problem?
5. Describe the cut known as "emince."
6. What is the most basic equipment used for fabricating meats?

What Went Wrong?

The chef asked the purveyor to give him a boneless loin of pork, but, when it was delivered, the loin was bone-in. No one in the kitchen knew what to do, and eventually the loin of pork had to be thrown away.

Chapter *12*

Poultry Fabrication

There are so many ways to prepare poultry of all sorts that it is certainly a good idea to learn to properly cut birds. This chapter focuses primarily on the ways that a chicken can be cut up for preparation. There is no reason that these same techniques could not be used on different birds, such as ducks, turkeys, capons, or pheasant.

After reading and studying this chapter, you should be able to:
1. Name the basic rules for working with poultry to prevent cross contamination.
2. Name and describe the tools needed for cutting up poultry.
3. Explain what is meant by disjointing poultry.
4. Describe the procedure for preparing a suprême.
5. Describe the steps necessary to cut a bird into halves, quarters, and eighths.
6. Describe a method for trussing a bird.

Matching

1. _____ Trussing
2. _____ Drumstick
3. _____ Free-range
4. _____ Keel bone
5. _____ Poultry shears

a. The cartilege found in the breast of birds.
b. Tying a bird into a neat shape for roasting.
c. The lower part of a bird's leg.
d. Scissors used to cut through small bones and joints on birds.
e. Birds that roam freely in an enclosed yard.

Multiple Choice

1. Poultry is often purchased whole because
   a. most restaurants roast birds whole, rather than cutting them into pieces.
   b. most poultry is relatively easy to cut into the shape and size needed, and any trim can be used for stocks, hors d'oeuvre, and other preparations.
   c. that is the only way it is available to restaurants; only supermarkets have precut poultry for sale.
   d. that is the tradition.

2. Cross-contamination from uncooked poultry can be avoided by making certain to
   a. unwrap and dispose of any plastic or styrofoam in contact with the birds upon delivery.
   b. store all uncooked birds in the freezer.
   c. clean and sanitize all tools and work surfaces before and after cutting the poultry, and be sure to store them in leakproof containers, below other foods so that they will not drip.
   d. allowing only one person in the kitchen to work with raw poultry.
3. A suprême of chicken has
   a. two wing joints and some of the rib cage still attached.
   b. no skin and no bones.
   c. skin still on, and a piece of the back still attached.
   d. no skin and no bones, with the exception of one wing joint.
4. The keel bone is found
   a. near the tail of the bird.
   b. in the rib cage, separating the two halves of the breast.
   c. in the thigh.
   d. in the giblet bag.
5. The legs can be separated from the body of the bird by
   a. making a cut between the breast and the thigh and then popping the joint that connects the leg to the body.
   b. simply pulling them away.
   c. ordering them separately.
   d. using a cleaver to cut through the joint.

True/False

1. _____ All birds are exactly like a chicken.

2. _____ The keel bone is often left attached to the breast when preparing a suprême.

3. _____ Trussing is a good technique to make certain that birds roast evenly, retain their moisture, and look attractive.

4. _____ Broilers and fryers are often cut into eighths and then panfried or prepared by other cooking methods.

5. _____ It is possible to completely remove the bones from the leg of a chicken or other poultry.

6. _____ Cornish game hens are always roasted whole. They are never cut up before they are served to the customer.

7. _____ The bones may be left intact for birds that are being grilled to help prevent shrinkage.

8. _____ It is very important to keep poultry under refrigeration when it is not being worked on.

Fill in the Blank

1. The part of the chef's knife used to cut through the end of the drumstick is the _____.
2. In order to bone out the leg of a bird, you should use the tip of your boning knife to cut along the _____.
3. A final (optional) step when halving a bird is to _____.
4. The first part of the bird that is cut away before continuing to cut the bird into halves or quarters is _____.
5. A boneless, skinless poultry breast with one wing joint still attached is known as a _____.
6. In order to make a bird compact, neat, and in a shape so that it will cook evenly and be attractive, it should be _____.

Discussion

1. Chicken is shown exclusively in this chapter. Why is that?
2. Name some of the benefits of buying whole birds. Name several uses for the "trim" and "waste." Why is it important to use this trim and waste?
3. Describe how to prepare ducks for restaurant service.
4. What pieces are available after a bird has been cut into eighths? What birds are generally cut up this way? What are some of the cooking techniques that might call for the birds to be cut into eighths?

What Went Wrong?

A restaurant has fried chicken on the menu, and it also serves many soups. The owner prefers to buy precut and prebreaded chicken and to purchase stock base for use in the soups. They also serve Buffalo wings as an appetizer. These, like the fried chicken, are purchased precut and pre-coated. One day, the accountant announces that there is simply not enough profit being made, and asks the owner to talk to the chef about ways to improve profit. What would you suggest?

Chapter 13

Fish and Shellfish Fabrication

Menu selections that are based on fish and shellfish are increasing in popularity all the time. The skills necessary to prepare fish for cooking are easy to learn. With continued practice, a chef can save money by purchasing fish that are not already filleted, shucked, or cut into steaks. It is also likely that a chef who can work with whole fish can increase profits by using the entire fish to prepare stocks, soups, forcemeats, terrines, and appetizers, in addition to the various entrées that might be on the menu.

After reading and studying this chapter, you should be able to:

1. Describe two ways to scale fish.
2. Name the major steps in preparing both flat and round fish into fillets (and related cuts) and steaks so that they can be made pan-ready.
3. Clean shrimp to remove the shells and the intestines.
4. Working with a cooking lobster, describe the procedure for cutting it in half, the procedure for removing the tail, and the three methods for removing lobster claw meat.
5. Clean and pick crayfish to remove the tail meat.
6. Clean soft-shelled crabs to prepare them for cooking.
7. Clean and open clams, oysters, and mussels.
8. Clean squid and octopus.
9. Clean sea urchins.
10. Skin an eel.

Matching

1. _____ Viscera
2. _____ Rack
3. _____ Beard
4. _____ Goujonette
5. _____ Quill
6. _____ Apron
7. _____ Pan-ready
8. _____ Needlenose pliers
9. _____ Tomalley
10. _____ Paupiette

a. The skeleton of a cepahlopod.
b. The fibers a mussel uses to attach itself to a mooring.
c. A skinless fish filled, rolled, and shallow-poached.
d. Used to remove pinbones from fish such as salmon.
e. Fish that has been scaled, gutted, and may have head and tail removed as well.
f. A lobster's liver.
g. A fish skeleton.
h. A small, finger-sized piece of fish fillet.
i. The flap on a soft-shelled crab's stomach.
j. Another term for the fish's guts.

Multiple Choice

1. The viscera (or guts) should be removed from a fish as soon as possible because
    a. they are inedible.
    b. the enzymes in the viscera could begin to break down the flesh rapidly, leading to spoilage.
    c. they are poisonous to man.
    d. the smell of the viscera could permeate the flesh.
2. In order to remove the intramuscular bones from a salmon and similar fish, you need to
    a. use a magnifying glass.
    b. run a finger down the center of each fillet, to locate the bones and then pull them out with needlenose pliers.
    c. make a V-shaped notch cut down the length of the fish.
    d. cut the fillet in half.
3. A flat fish has
    a. both eyes on the same side of its head.
    b. pale white skin on both sides.
    c. a high fat content.
    d. only two fillets.
4. The skin should be removed from a fish
    a. before it is boned.
    b. before it is gutted.
    c. after the fins and head have been removed.
    d. after the fillet has been cut away from the bones.
5. The chef will usually want to use
    a. a rigid filleting knife to fillet a salmon.
    b. a boning knife to fillet a salmon.
    c. both a flexible filleting knife and a chef's knife to fillet a salmon.
    d. all of the above.
6. A paupiette is usually
    a. left flat, breaded, and pan-fried.
    b. rolled into a cylinder, perhaps with a stuffing, and then poached.
    c. served with Hollandaise.
    d. the term used to describe a fish that is not fresh.
7. Mussels should be carefully
    a. stored in cold water.
    b. shucked to serve on the half shell.
    c. cooked to an internal temperature of 170°F.
    d. checked to be sure that they are live and that the shells are not filled with mud.

True/False

1. _____ Octopus and squid do not have to be tough and rubbery if they are properly prepared.

2. _____ The tomalley and the roe should always be discarded because they cannot be eaten.

3. _____ A crayfish's intestine can only be removed after the crayfish is cooked.

4. _____ There is a bubble filled with a foul-tasting green liquid in a soft-shelled crab that must be removed before cooking.

5. _____ Shucked clams and oysters are always poached before serving.

6. _____ Most flat fish cannot be cut into steaks; halibut is an exception to this general statement.

7. _____ The best way to cut a tranche of salmon is to hold the knife so that it will make vertical cuts.

8. _____ It is usually easier to remove the first two fillets from a flat fish; the second two will be a little more difficult.

Fill in the Blank

1. Another name for intramuscular bones found in salmon is _____.
2. When you remove the meat from the tail of the crayfish and remove any bits of shell, you are _____.
3. The name for the body of a cephalophod is the _____.
4. A protective device used by squid and octopus to hide themselves when they escape from predators, as well as an ingredient in special dishes such as black rice, is the _____.
5. The part of the sea urchin that is eaten is the orange-colored _____.
6. The name for the arms attached to the body of a cephalopod is _____.

Discussion

1. What are the best reasons for learning to properly clean and prepare a wide variety of fish and shellfish?
2. Name several different cuts or menu items that can be prepared from a fillet of fish.
3. Some of the most popular fish are cut into steaks and prepared on the grill. Name some fish that are suitable for cutting into steaks.
4. Briefly describe the method for gutting and filleting both flat and round fish.

What Went Wrong?

The fish purveyor arrives to say that there is no lemon sole available today. However, there is a good buy on orange roughy. The chef decides simply not to purchase any fish, even though there is a lemon sole entrée on the menu. Explain why you think he might have been unwilling or unable to purchase the orange roughy, and what the consequences of his decision might be.

Chapter 14

Mise en Place

This chapter introduces the concept of mise en place (total preparedness) and explains how to correctly hold and use a knife, as well as the techniques to prepare a number of basic preparations required in the production of other dishes or as part of the set-up for a station. After reading and studying this chapter you should be able to:

1. Understand different ways to hold a knife, depending on the particular task.
2. Identify all the basic vegetable cuts and their uses.
3. Zest citrus fruit and peel tomatoes and peppers.
4. Prepare basic aromatic and flavoring combinations, such as mirepoix, matignon, bouquet garni, sachet d'épices, and marinades.
5. Understand the method and use of the following thickeners: slurry, roux, beurre manié, liaison, and gelatin.
6. Prepare basic ingredients and appareils, such as clarified butter, rendering fats, duxelles, pesto, persillade, and pâte à choux.
7. Know the following basic cooking and miscellaneous techniques: separating eggs, whipping egg whites, whipping cream, folding whipped items into a base appareil, use of a bain-marie/water bath, and cutting parchment liners.

Matching

1. __E__ Zest

2. __D__ ~~~~ Liaison

3. __H__ Tomato concassé

4. __A__ Matignon

5. __K__ Roux

6. __C__ Marinade

7. __I__ Mirepoix

8. __F__ Beurre manié

9. __L__ Duxelles

a. An edible mirepoix intended to be served as part of a finished dish.

b. A starch dissolved in a cold liquid.

c. Used to flavor foods before they are cooked; originally used to preserve and tenderize.

d. A mixture of both egg yolks and cream, used to both thicken and enrich sauces and soups.

e. The outer portion of a citrus fruit peel or rind, used to add color, texture, and flavor.

f. Equal parts by weight of uncooked whole butter and flour, used to thicken sauces and stews.

g. A flavoring ingredient made by fastening a bay leaf to a onion with a whole clove.

h. Peeled, seeded, and coarsely chopped tomatoes.

i. A combination of rough, chopped aromatic vegetables, used to flavor stocks, soups, braises, and stews.

10. __B__ Slurry

11. __J__ Bouquet garni

12. __M__ Onion brulé

13. __N__ Sachet d'épices

14. __G__ Onion piqué

j. A combination of herbs and vegetables, tied in a bundle, used to flavor savory preparations.

k. Cooked fat and flour; often prepared in advance in large quantities.

l. A mixture of finely chopped and sautéed mushrooms, used as a flavoring, stuffing, or coating.

m. A charred onion used in stocks and consommes to provide a golden brown color.

n. A "bag of spices" that is removed and discarded after enough flavor has been given.

Multiple Choice

1. Adding a portion of a hot liquid to a liaison to keep it from "scrambling" is called
   a. rendering.
   b. tempering.
   c. clarifying.
   d. dissolving.
   e. blanching.
2. A mixture of breadcrumbs, minced parsley and garlic, used as a coating for roasted or grilled items is called
   a. paté à choux.
   b. duxelles.
   c. pesto.
   d. matignon.
   e. persillade.
3. What is the difference between a matignon and a mirepoix?
   a. Mirepoix is rough cut, whereas matignon is uniformly cut.
   b. Mirepoix is strained from a preparation and a matignon is left in to be eaten as part of the dish.
   c. Matignon contains bacon or ham, whereas mirepoix is meatless.
   d. The vegetables in a matignon are peeled, but in a mirepoix they may be unpeeled.
   e. All of the above.
4. A mixture of ingredients used as one component in preparing a given dish is called
   a. mise en place.
   b. mirepoix.
   c. rondelle.
   d. fermière.
   e. appareil.
5. A food item cut into a brunoise will have what dimensions?
   a. $1/8'' \times 1/8'' \times 1$ to $2''$.
   b. $1/8'' \times 1/8'' \times 1/8''$.
   c. Seven 2-inch sides.
   d. $1/2'' \times 1/2'' \times 1/8''$.
   e. None of the above.
6. A mixture of an herb and oil that is puréed until smooth is called
   a. persillade.
   b. paté à choux.
   c. pesto.
   d. bouquet garni.
   e. none of the above.

True/False

1. __F__ Chiffonade is a cut used primarily for root vegetables.
2. __T__ In order to obtain the maximum volume from whipped egg whites, all traces of fat must be eliminated.
3. __T__ The zest of a lemon includes only the brightly colored portion of the skin.
4. __T X✓__ Most marinades are acid- and oil-based liquids.
5. __T__ Matignon is occasionally referred to as "edible mirepoix."

Fill in the Blank

1. __Sugar__ or __Acidic__ ingredients will inhibit the gelling proprieties of gelatin.
2. When combining roux with a liquid, be sure that their individual temperatures are __different__.
3. Clarified butter can be heated to a higher temperature than whole butter without burning or breaking down because the __milk solids__, which scorch easily, have been removed.
4. __Reduction__ is a process that removes some or all of the liquid and not only thickens, but concentrates the liquids flavor.
5. Ideally, a liaison should be added to a sauce or soup __before service__.

Discussion

1. List the dimensions for the following vegetable cuts:
   a. Fine julienne. $\frac{1}{16} \times \frac{1}{16} \times 2$
   b. Julienne/allumette. $\frac{1}{8} \times \frac{1}{8} \times 2$
   c. Batonnet. $\frac{1}{4} \times \frac{1}{4} \times 2$
   d. Brunoise. $\frac{1}{8} \times \frac{1}{8} \times \frac{1}{8}$
   e. Small dice. $\frac{1}{4} \times \frac{1}{4} \times \frac{1}{4}$
   f. Medium dice. $\frac{1}{3} \times \frac{1}{3} \times \frac{1}{3}$
   g. Large dice. $\frac{3}{4} \times \frac{3}{4} \times \frac{3}{4}$
   h. Paysanne. $\frac{1}{2} \times \frac{1}{2} \times \frac{1}{8}$
   i. Tourné. 7-2 inch side
   j. Chiffonade. very fine
2. Briefly describe the four methods for peeling sweet and hot peppers.
3. What is the difference between a onion piqué and a onion brulé?
4. Briefly explain how to prepare tomato concassé.
5. What is a bain-marie, and how is it used?
6. Name the particular knife cuts that are used especially for long, cylindrical vegetables, such as parsnips, carrots, and cucumbers.
7. Briefly describe the two methods for clarifying butter.
8. Briefly describe the method for whipping egg whites.
9. What is the purpose of covering items with parchment paper when cooking?
10. Briefly describe the procedure for thickening a liquid with gelatin.

What Went Wrong?

As the evening service period reaches its peak, some of the line cooks are having difficulty getting entreées and side dishes ready on time. They haven't got enough of a number of things. Describe what they should have assembled as mise en place. Name as many items as you can.

Chapter 15

Stocks

With this chapter, the student begins to apply actual cooking techniques that will have a broad application in the professional kitchen. Stocks are fundamental to the work of the chef, and the ability to produce good, flavorful stocks of the best quality is an excellent starting place for building proficiency. After reading and studying this chapter, the reader will be able to:

1. Identify the characteristics of a stock.
2. List and describe the different types of stocks.
3. Describe the three uses for stocks.
4. Understand the basic components of a stock.
5. Discuss various ways to prepare bones before using them in a stock.
6. Understand the basic preparation method for a stock.
7. Evaluate the quality of a stock.

Matching

1. _____ Remouillage

2. _____ Essence

3. _____ Fumet

4. _____ Brown stock

5. _____ Broth or bouillon

6. _____ Glace

7. _____ White stock

8. _____ Court bouillon

a. An amber liquid made by first browning poultry, beef, veal, or game bones and aromatics.

b. A clear, relatively colorless liquid made by simmering poultry, beef, or fish bones and the appropriate aromatics.

c. Is essentially the same as a fumet, but uses highly aromatic products, such as celery and morels.

d. An aromatic vegetable broth that frequently includes wine and/or vinegar.

e. A stock reduced to a jelly-like or syrupy consistency, concentrating the flavors.

f. A highly flavored stock, generally made from fish bones.

g. A stock made from bones that have already been used—a rewetting.

h. A liquid that results from simmering meats.

Multiple Choice

1. What is the best choice of liquid for the most richly flavored stock?
   a. Water.
   b. Remouillage.
   c. Court bouillon.
   d. Glace.
   e. None of the above.
2. Ingredients or combinations of ingredients such as herbs, root vegetables, a sachet d'épices, and boquet garnis are used to give a dish a special flavor. They may be referred to by the general term
   a. mirepoix.
   b. essence.
   c. remouillage.
   d. aromatics.
   e. none of the above.
3. Fish fumet and court bouillon should have a mirepoix that has been
   a. left unpeeled.
   b. cut into large chunks.
   c. blanched.
   d. cut small.
   e. caramelized.
4. A stock's clarity is better preserved if the major flavoring ingredients and mirepoix are
   a. disturbed as little as possible.
   b. always browned.
   c. stirred every half hour.
   d. boiled rapidly.
   e. all of the above.
5. What generally is done to frozen bones to remove impurities when making a white stock?
   a. The bones are sweated.
   b. The bones are browned in a hot oven until they are brown.
   c. The bones are cut into smaller pieces than normal.
   d. The bones are blanched, starting with cold water.
   e. b and d.

True/False

1. _____ Pincé is the process of lightly browning a tomato product.

2. _____ Once a finished stock is put in an appropriate container, it is not necessary to remove any fat from the stock surface until after it is thoroughly chilled.

3. _____ A freshly made stock is usually more expensive than prepared bases.

4. _____ All stocks are usually started with hot water.

5. _____ Court bouillon may be used as a soup or as the basis of other soups, stews, and braises.

Fill in the Blank

1. The _____ present in fish bones and shellfish shells can take on an unacceptable flavor if allowed to cook too long.
2. Skimming removes impurities that are trapped by the _____ that rises to the top of a stock.

3. White stocks should remain relatively clear and not have a _____.
4. _____ may replace water in the making of a stock.
5. Not only do bones for stock need to be the correct size, they also may need to be _____, _____, or _____.

Discussion

1. What are the three major uses for stocks?
2. List and describe the three major components of a stock.
3. What three things may be done to prepare bones before they are made into a stock? Explain each point.
4. Describe the basic preparation method for a stock.
5. What four properties are evaluated when judging the quality of a stock?
6. List and describe four variations of a brown stock.
7. Why are stocks considered a fonds de cuisine?
8. What is an estouffade, and how is it used?

What Went Wrong?

The stock prepared yesterday is pulled from the cooler to prepare a soup. The sous chef is suspicious that something might not be right. It seems cloudy and has a peculiar smell that becomes more intense as the stock is heated.

Chapter 16

Soups

This chapter introduces the correct methods for preparing soups, and groups them into two basic categories: Clear soups and thick soups. There is also discussion of specialty and national soups, such as chowders, gumbos, and minestrones. After reading and studying this chapter, you should be able to:

1. Understand the basic ingredients and their functions in a soup.
2. Understand how to properly cook, finish, garnish, reheat, adjust consistency, and degrease clear and thick soups.
3. Prepare and evaluate the quality of clear soups, including consommés, broths, and clear vegetable soups.
4. Prepare and evaluate the quality of thick soups, including purées, cream soups, and bisques.
5. Prepare and evaluate the quality of cold soups and speciality soups, including chowders, gumbos, minestrone, and others.
6. Serve hot and cold soups in the correct manner.

Matching

1. _____ Bisque

    a. A vegetable soup, usually containing pasta or beans.

2. _____ Clear vegetable soup

    b. A strong crystal clear broth or stock that has been clarified.

3. _____ Gumbo

    c. A somewhat thick and course soup based on dried peas, lentils, or beans or other starchy vegetables.

4. _____ Consommé

    d. A chilled soup based on raw vegetables.

5. _____ Purée

    e. Based on a clear broth or stock with the vegetables cut into an appropriate and uniform size.

6. _____ Cream soup

    f. A rich, flavorful soup based on meats prepared with water or stock.

7. _____ Garbure

    g. A thick soup invariably containing potatoes.

8. _____ Broth

    h. Made with a dark roux, okra, and/or gumbo file.

9. _____ Gazpacho

    i. Béchamel- or velouté-based soup, finished with cream or a liaison.

10. _____ Minestrone

    j. Traditionally based on crustaceans and shares characteristics with both purees and cream soups.

11. _____ Chowder

    k. A soup where some or all of the ingredients have been puréed. May also include starchy ingredients, giving the finished soup more body than a clear soup.

Multiple Choice

1. The process of enriching a broth or stock and transforming it into a crystal-clear consommé is called
   a. degreasing.
   b. clarifying.
   c. spatzli.
   d. skimming.
   e. none of the above.

2. Which of the following soups are *not* considered clear soups?
   a. Broth.
   b. Consommé.
   c. Clear vegetable soup.
   d. Bisque.
   e. None of the above.

3. A vegetable-based bisque is prepared in the same manner as a
   a. chowder.
   b. vichyssoise.
   c. consommé.
   d. cream soup.
   e. none of the above.

4. When is the best time to add cream to a cream soup?
   a. Immediately after it is puréed.
   b. When the main flavoring components are added.
   c. After it has come to a full boil.
   d. Just before service.
   e. Any of the above.

5. Because a velvety-smooth texture is critical to all cream soups, what must be done?
   a. Use a consommé instead of a stock.
   b. Use a velouté base as opposed to a béchamel.
   c. Strain the soup.
   d. Finish the cream soup with a liaison.
   e. None of the above.

True/False

1. _____ Mirepoix is an essential ingredient in all soups.

2. _____ Broths and clear vegetable soups characteristically have some droplets of fat on the surface.

3. _____ Simmering a prepared consommé makes it easier to lift away the congealed fat surface.

4. _____ A bisque that is properly made will have a slightly grainy texture.

5. _____ Thick soups, especially creams, purees, and bisques, should be reheated very quickly to avoid scorching.

Fill in the Blank

1. Clear vegetable soups should have a full flavor and be somewhat _____ than broths.
2. A cloudy consommé is most often the result of _____ the soup.
3. Cream soups should have the approximate body, consistency, and texture of _____.
4. The major distinction between broths and stocks is that broths are intended to be served _____.
5. _____ form the basis of most soups.

Discussion

1. What are the three basic ingredients in a soup?
2. Describe the procedure for finishing and garnishing soups.
3. Describe the procedure for reheating thick and clear soups.
4. What are the three basic types of soups? Give two examples of each.
5. Briefly describe what garnishing can accomplish in soups.
6. What qualities should a well-prepared broth have?
7. Briefly describe how a consommé is clarified.
8. What qualities should a well-prepared consommé have?
9. What qualities should a well-prepared clear vegetable soup have?
10. Cream of vegetable soup follows one of two methods. Briefly describe both of these methods.
11. What three options does one have for thickening a cream soup?
12. What qualities should a well-prepared cream soup have?
13. What qualities should a well-prepared purée soup have?
14. Briefly describe the history of bisques. Also discuss some different techniques that chefs use to prepare bisques.
15. What qualities should a well-prepared bisque have?
16. List and describe four types of "specialty" or "national" soups.
17. Discuss the variety of ways that cold soups can be prepared.
18. Give the method for proper service of hot and cold soups.

What Went Wrong?

1. Even after clarification, the consommé is cloudy.
2. A cream soup is very thick, with a starchy and almost scorched flavor.

Chapter 17

Sauces

In this chapter we will explain and evaluate the grand and contemporary sauces and modern sauce-making techniques. After reading and studying the chapter, you should be able to:

1. List and describe the five purposes that sauces serve in modern cooking.
2. Understand the proper selection of a sauce, depending on specific uses.
3. List and describe the four grand sauces and hollandaise sauce.
4. Understand the method of preparation for the grand sauces, hollandaise, contemporary sauces, and compound butters.
5. Evaluate the quality of all grand and contemporary sauces.
6. Identify the primary factors that distinguish contemporary sauces from the grand sauces.
7. List and describe a number of alternatives to traditional sauces and how they can be used in place of traditional sauces.

Matching

1. _____ Grand sauce

2. _____ Espagnole sauce

3. _____ Demi-glace

4. _____ Jus lié

5. _____ Tomato sauce

6. _____ Béchamel

7. _____ Velouté

8. _____ Hollandaise

9. _____ Coulis

10. _____ Beurre blanc

a. A clear, translucent sauce made from stock, usually thickened with a modified starch.

b. A white sauce made by thickening milk with a white roux.

c. A sauce in which butter forms an emulsion with a reduction (traditionally, the cuisson).

d. Equal parts Espagnole sauce and brown veal stock, reduced by half.

e. An emulsion sauce made when clarified or melted butter is suspended in partially cooked egg yolks.

f. A grand sauce made by simmering tomatoes with stock, aromatics, and other ingredients and then pureeing.

g. Referred to as the mother sauces, to indicate that from these basic sauces many others are created.

h. Brown stock thickened with a pale roux and seasoned with aromatics and tomato.

i. White stock thickened with a pale roux.

j. Generally indicates a sauce that is a purée of a vegetable.

Multiple Choice

1. One of the fundamental benefits of the grand sauces is that
   a. they take a short time to prepare.
   b. they can be prepared in advance and held in large quantities at the proper temperature.
   c. they can all be made with light stock.
   d. any grand sauce can be served with any meat or fish.
   e. none of the above.

2. A hollandaise sauce is not always considered a grand sauce because
   a. it cannot be made in advance and cannot be used to prepare a variety of derivatives.
   b. it does not require a roux.
   c. it can only be served with vegetables and egg dishes.
   d. it requires little time or effort to prepare.
   e. all of the above.

3. The primary factor distinguishing contemporary sauces from grand sauces is
   a. contemporary sauces tend to be lighter in body and color.
   b. grand sauces usually require more time to prepare.
   c. many contemporary sauces are updated versions of grand sauces.
   d. none of the above.
   e. all of the above.

4. A demi-glace is made from
   a. equal parts Espagnole sauce and white stock reduced by half.
   b. equal parts brown veal stock and velouté reduced by half.
   c. equal parts tomato sauce and Espagnole sauce reduced by half.
   d. any of the above.
   e. none of the above.

5. A velouté sauce is based on what stock?
   a. Chicken stock.
   b. Fish stock
   c. Veal stock
   d. Any white stock.
   e. Any brown stock.

True/False

1. _____ Espagnole sauce is an essential ingredient in demi-glace.

2. _____ The procedure for holding a beurre blanc sauce is the same as for hollandaise sauce.

3. _____ A vin blanc sauce is a derivative of a Beurre Blanc Sauce.

4. _____ The purpose of a sauce is to complement, never contrast with, a particular food.

5. _____ Cold vinaigrettes and mayonnaise may be used as a sauce for hot sautéed items or as a marinade.

Fill in the Blank

1. When the components of a hollandaise sauce are combined in the proper ratio, the sauce flavor will be predominately that of _____.
2. Beurre blancs are suitable for foods that have been _____.
3. _____ is a white sauce made by thickening milk with a white roux.
4. Tomato sauce should have a rich, tomato flavor with no trace of _____.
5. _____ is often used to deglaze pans to create sauces that are specifically tailored to sautés or roasts.

Discussion

1. List and briefly describe the five purposes of sauces.
2. Describe the three points of proper sauce selection.
3. Why do some chefs prefer melted butter to clarified butter when making a hollandaise sauce?
4. List the four grand sauces.
5. What qualities should the following sauces have when properly prepared?
   a. Demi-glace.
   b. Velouté.
   c. Béchamel.
   d. Tomato.
   e. Hollandaise.
   f. Beurre blanc.
   g. Jus lié.
6. Discuss the best way to hold a hollandaise sauce once it is made.
7. List some miscellaneous sauces that can be used in a contemporary kitchen.
8. What is a compound butter and how is it used?
9. What is the difference between a demi-glace and a glace de viande?
10. Briefly describe the procedure for preparing the following sauces:
    a. Espagnole.
    b. Demi-glace.
    c. Velouté.
    d. Béchamel.
    e. Tomato.
    f. Hollandaise.
    g. Jus lié.
    h. Beurre blanc.

What Went Wrong?

1. While preparing a beurre blanc, the sauté chef notices that the sauce has become thick and it is difficult to add more butter.
2. The hollandaise has a curdled appearance, and there appears to be some scrambling.

Chapter 18

Dry-heat Cooking without Fats or Oils

This chapter introduces and explains techniques for cooking foods by exposing them to direct heat (radiant heat or convection). Although the title of this chapter may seem to indicate that this is cooking devoid of fats or oils, they are used occasionally to give the food a particular flavor, as well as to aid in browning. After reading and studying this chapter, you should be able to:

1. Properly grill and broil foods.
2. Define the various terms that apply to grilling and broiling.
3. Identify and use the correct tools required for grilling and broiling.
4. Properly roast and poêlé foods.
5. Define the various terms that apply to poêléing and roasting.
6. Identify and use the correct tools used in roasting and poêléing.
7. Properly determine doneness in roasted foods, allowing for carry-over cooking.
8. Properly carve roasted foods for service.
9. Discuss the advantages of including grilled, roasted, and poêléed items on contemporary menus.

Matching

1. _____ Barbecue

2. _____ Barding

3. _____ Pan gravy

4. _____ A point

5. _____ Broiling

6. _____ Smoke-roasting

a. A technique used to cook foods where the heat source is located below the food.

b. When roasting, this sauce is made from the accumulated drippings in the pan.

c. A French term usually applied to foods that are cooked just to the point of doneness, and no more.

d. A style of grilling, often, a sauce is repeatedly brushed on the surface of the food to give additional flavor, color, and sheen.

e. A technique that cooks foods by surrounding them with dry air in a closed environment.

f. A technique used to cook foods on the top of the stove in a cast iron or other heat-resistant metal pan over intense heat.

7. _____ Au jus

8. _____ Pan broiling

9. _____ Grilling

10. _____ Poêléing

11. _____ Carry-over cooking

12. _____ Spit-roasting

13. _____ Roasting

g. A type of cooking where the heat source is located above the item to be cooked.

h. Meats allowed to cook in their own juices in a covered vessel on a bed of aromatic vegetables.

i. This technique of roasting involves placing the food on a rod that is turned either manually or with a motor.

j. A type of cooking technique where foods are roasted in a closed vessel along with hardwood chips that have been heated to the point at which they smoke.

k. A sauce used in roasting that is made with a roux that incorporates the fat rendered from the roast.

l. The action that allows roasted foods to continue to cook after they have been removed from the oven.

m. A technique used in roasting, where the item is wrapped in thin sheets of fatback or caul fat to keep the item moist.

Multiple Choice

1. The original form of roasting and the oldest form of cookery is called
   a. pan-roasting.
   b. spit-roasting.
   c. barbecuing.
   d. poêléing.
   e. grilling.
2. A matignon, also called an edible mirepoix, is often used with
   a. poêléing.
   b. barding.
   c. pan-roasting.
   d. pan-broiling.
   e. all of the above.
3. Foods cooked by roasting, grilling, broiling, or poêléing
   a. should be left in large pieces for even cooking.
   b. are always cooked and served rare.
   c. should be naturally tender.
   d. should always have a smoky flavor.
   e. a and c only.
4. Allowing an item to rest after it has roasted
   a. will give the cook time to prepare the rest of the meal.
   b. is an optional technique.
   c. stops the carry-over cooking of the roast.
   d. redistributes the juices that have accumulated in the center of the roast.
   e. none of the above.
5. Broiling, barbecuing, and pan-broiling are all forms of
   a. roasting.
   b. pan-roasting.
   c. poêléing.
   d. broiling.
   e. none of the above.

True/False

1. _____ When dry-heat cooking without fats or oils, stocks may be used during the cooking process to insure tenderness and moistness.

2. _____ The most often used test for doneness in grilled foods is touch.

3. _____ When grilling and broiling white meats, they should be cooked through (à point), but not overcooked.

4. _____ Poêléing is also known as pan-broiling.

5. _____ Roasting and poêléing require longer cooking times because these techniques are most frequently used with large cuts of meat or whole birds or fish.

Fill in the Blank

1. When grilling and broiling, beef cooked _____ has a very deep maroon color.
2. A piece of meat should be removed from the oven when the internal temperature is _____ than the desired doneness. It will complete cooking through _____.
3. The most reliable method for determining doneness in roasted items is to use an _____.
4. Poêléing is most often associated with _____ and _____.
5. Unlike roasted items, which may be cooked to various degrees of doneness, poêléed items are cooked until _____.

Discussion

1. What are the two major factors in successfully using dry-heat techniques without fats or oils?
2. What types of meat are best suited for broiling, roasting, and poêléing? Explain your answer.
3. What are some of the characteristics of grilled foods?
4. Where is the heat source located in broiling and grilling?
5. Briefly describe pan-broiling and barbecuing.
6. What is the purpose of marinating broiled or grilled items before cooking them?
7. What is the purpose of mentally dividing a grill or broiler into zones?
8. Describe the procedure for making crosshatch marks or grilled or broiled foods.
9. Briefly describe how to determine doneness with broiled and grilled items. Include red meats, white meats, and fish and shellfish.
10. What three things should you use as gauges when determining quality for grilled and broiled foods?
11. Briefly describe the procedure for grilling.
12. Briefly describe roasting. How does it differ from grilling?
13. What is spit-roasting and how is it done?
14. What is barding and why is it done?
15. What is smoke-roasting and how is it accomplished?
16. Discuss the various sauces that can be prepared from the drippings in roasted foods.
17. What is carry-over cooking? Give an example. What is the difference in carry-over cooking between a quail and a steamship round?
18. In roasting, what is the purpose of mirepoix in the cooking process?
19. What is the purpose of resting roasted items before carving them? What would happen to a roasted item if you carved it without a resting period?
20. Briefly describe the procedure for roasting.
21. What is the best way in determining doneness in roasted foods?
22. What three factors are used in evaluating the quality of roasted items?
23. Briefly describe poêléing. What types of meats are best suited for this cooking technique?
24. What is the purpose of adding butter or a matignon during poêléing?
25. Briefly describe the method for poêléing.

26. When poêléing, what is the purpose of "seizing" the item?
27. How does one determine doneness in poêléed foods?
28. What are the three important characteristics used when evaluating the quality of poêléed foods?
29. Why are grilling, roasting, and poêléing potentially very good items to have on any menu?

What Went Wrong?

1. The roast looks good, but, when it is sliced, the meat is dry, rubbery, and tough. The jus lié prepared from the drippings has a harsh, bitter flavor.
2. The chef experimented with grilling a halved duck. The end result was a mixture of success and failure.

Chapter 19

Dry-heat Cooking with Fats and Oils

This chapter introduces and explains the cooking techniques that rely on fat or oil to act as the cooking medium. As the amount and temperature of the oil are altered in relation to the quantity of food being cooked, different effects are achieved. After reading and studying this chapter, you should be able to:

1. Select and prepare items to be sautéed.
2. Prepare stir-fried foods.
3. Properly panfry foods.
4. Set up and use the standard breading procedure.
5. Deep-fry foods, using both the basket, double-basket, and swimming techniques.
6. Understand what is meant by "smoking point," and how it applies to all cooking techniques that rely on fats and oils as the cooking medium.
7. Properly select and maintain fats and oils used for deep-frying.

Matching

1. _____ Recovery time

    a. To release the reduced drippings from the bottom of a pan by adding a small amount of liquid and stirring until the drippings lift away.

2. _____ Panfrying

    b. Finishing a sauce with whole butter at the end of the cooking process.

3. _____ Monté au beurre

    c. The process of dusting food items in flour, dipping in eggwash, and then coating with any number of breadings.

4. _____ Sauté

    d. The point at which fats and oils smoke, thus indicating the point at which they break down.

5. _____ Tempura

    e. A technique that cooks bite-size pieces of meat or fish quickly in a small amount of very hot oil.

6. _____ Smoking point

    f. A cooking method involving breaded foods cooked in a moderate amount of fat or oil.

7. _____ Standard breading procedure

    g. The technique of cooking food very quickly in a small amount of fat.

8. ____ Deep-frying		h.	The term used to describe foods that are cooked to order.

8. ____ Deep-frying

9. ____ Stir-frying

10. ____ A la minute

11. ____ Deglaze

h. The term used to describe foods that are cooked to order.

i. A Japanese style of deep-frying, in which items are coated with a thin batter that becomes very crisp and lacy as it fries.

j. A technique that cooks foods by submerging them in hot fat or oil.

k. This measures the amount of time it takes the oil to return to the proper temperature after an item is cooked.

Multiple Choice

1. Sauces served with panfried items
   a. are always made from the fond left in the pan.
   b. are always made separately.
   c. are made by deglazing the pan with jus and monté au beurre.
   d. are never used because the item is breaded.
   e. none of the above.

2. What purpose does a sauce serve with sautéed foods?
   a. Adds moisture that counteracts dryness resulting from the sautéing process.
   b. Captures the food's flavor that is lost during cooking.
   c. Introduces additional flavor.
   d. a and c, but not b.
   e. All of the above.

3. Certain types of deep-fried foods, in order to develop a good crust, need to be fully submerged in hot oil for a fairly long time. Which deep-frying technique would be the best to use?
   a. Basket method.
   b. Swimming method.
   c. Double-basket method.
   d. Blanching.
   e. Any of the above.

4. Food items to be stir-fried are
   a. cut into portion-size pieces.
   b. usually breaded, using the standard breading procedure.
   c. always blanched to shorten their cooking time.
   d. cut into bite-size pieces, which acts to tenderize the food.
   e. none of the above.

5. The most important considerations in choosing an oil for deep-frying are
   a. neutral flavor and color and low smoke point.
   b. fatty acids, flavor, and glycerin.
   c. well-developed flavor and color and a high smoke point.
   d. neutral flavor and color and a high smoke point.
   e. none of the above.

True/False

1. ____ All panfried foods should be cooked through (a point).

2. ____ Only naturally tender foods should be sautéed, and after sautéing, the product should remain tender and moist.

3. ____ Peanut oil, because of its flavor and high smoking point, is traditionally used for stir-frying.

4. _____ When deep-frying, a rendered fat, such as lard, may be used to create a special flavor.

5. _____ The object of sautéing is to produce a flavorful exterior, resulting from proper browning.

Fill in the Blank

1. When deep-fat frying, discard the oil if it becomes rancid, smokes below_____ , or foams excessively.

2. _____ indicates that food was sautéed at an overly low temperature or that the pan was too crowded.

3. Stir-frying, generally associated with Asian styles of cooking, shares many similarities with _____.

4. Whereas a sautéed item is lightly dusted with flour and quickly cooked over high heat in _____ amount of oil, a panfried food is usually coated with batter or bread and is cooked in a _____ amount of oil.

5. With the exception of tempura, which should be light gold in color, most deep-fried foods should have a _____ color.

Discussion

1. What types of foods are best suited for sautéing?
2. What three purposes does a sauce serve with sautéed items?
3. What cooking technique shares many similarities with sautéing?
4. Briefly describe any prepreparation needed for sautéed food items.
5. Why is it important to acquire a good seal on the outside of sautéed food items?
6. Briefly describe the cooking medium needed for sautéing.
7. Describe how to determine doneness with sautéed foods.
8. Briefly describe the method for sautéing.
9. What three things are used to evaluate quality in a sautéed food item?
10. What is the proper color for sautéed white and red meats when they are done cooking?
11. Why does meat used for stir-frying not have to be as tender as meat used for sautéing?
12. Describe the cooking medium used for stir-frying.
13. What optional components can be used when stir-frying?
14. Briefly describe the method for thickening sauces served with stir-fried items.
15. Why is it important for the meat to be dry and the cooking oil to be very hot when stir-frying?
16. Briefly describe the method for stir-frying.
17. How do you evaluate quality with stir-fried foods?
18. What are some of the differences between sautéing and panfrying?
19. Why is a sauce not made in the pan with panfried foods?
20. Briefly describe the cooking medium with panfried foods.
21. What is a standard breading procedure? Why is it used?
22. Why would you not stuff an item too full before cooking it?
23. Why would you chill a breaded item after it has gone through the standard breading procedure?
24. Why do you not stack foods that have gone through the standard breading procedure?
25. In general, how far up the food item should the cooking medium go when panfrying?
26. What visual clue can be used to tell when the cooking medium is hot enough to panfry?
27. Why is it important to acquire a good seal on the breading when panfrying?
28. Why should you not use a fork when panfrying?
29. Why would a panfried item be finished in the oven to complete its cooking?
30. How is doneness determined with panfried foods?
31. What characteristics are evaluated with panfried foods?
32. Briefly describe the method for panfrying a food item.

33. What is probably the biggest difference between deep-fat frying and sautéing or panfrying?
34. What purpose does a coating serve with deep-fried foods?
35. Briefly describe the following deep-fat–frying terms:
    a. Swimming method.
    b. Basket method.
    c. Double-basket method.
    d. Recovery time.
    e. Smoking point.
    f. Blanching.
36. What types of oils are best suited for deep-fat frying?
37. List and briefly describe the ten steps to prolong deep-fat–frying oils.
38. What mise en place can be done to foods to be deep-fried?
39. Briefly describe the cooking medium for deep-fat frying.
40. When deep-fat frying, what will happen to food that is added to fat that has not reached the proper temperature?
41. How do you determine doneness with deep-fried foods?
42. How do you evaluate quality in deep-fried foods?
43. Briefly describe the method for deep-fat frying foods.

What Went Wrong?

1. A platter of fried chicken is returned to the kitchen. Upon examination, it appears pale in color and soggy, and some of the pieces are not properly cooked through.
2. One of the evening's specials is a chicken croquette. Several customers have ordered it, but the first three orders have been returned to the kitchen because they taste like fish, are nearly black in color, and the coating has a bitter taste. The chef noticed when the first orders were fired that there was a great deal of foam and smoking. The special is deleted from the menu immediately, of course, and the guests who received the unacceptable croquettes are compensated.
3. One of the assistants to the sauté chef is asked to get the tenderloin of beef from the cooler, and then slice it into 6-ounce portions. The first order that is prepared that evening seems to be shrinking too much as it cooks, and it doesn't look exactly right. When it is cut open (the sauté chef is not willing to send it out that way), it is very tough.

Chapter 20

Moist-heat Cooking

This chapter introduces the techniques that cook food through the means of moist heat. By varying the amount of liquid, regulating the cooking speed correctly, and employing a number of special techniques, different results can be achieved. After reading and studying this chapter, you should be able to:

1. Properly steam foods.
2. Properly prepare foods en papillote.
3. Properly poach foods that are completely submerged in a poaching liquid.
4. Properly shallow poach foods.
5. Determine doneness correctly and evaluate the quality of foods prepared by each of the techniques discussed in this chapter.

Matching

1. _____ Poaching

2. _____ Steaming

3. _____ En papillote

4. _____ Boiling

5. _____ Shallow poaching

6. _____ Simmering

a. Food that is partially submerged in liquid and cooked by a combination of steam and liquid bath.

b. A variation of steaming in which the item is creased in parchment paper and cooked in a hot oven.

c. A cooking technique for less tender cuts that cooks them in liquid between 185°F–200°F.

d. To cook foods by completely submerging them in liquid at 180°F–185°F.

e. This method cooks foods by surrounding them with a vapor bath.

f. Vigorous cooking method applied to very few foods because of its potential to cause meats, fish, and poultry to become tough and stringy.

Multiple Choice

1. Poaching and simmering are techniques that call for a food to be
   a. cooked quickly in a small amount of liquid.
   b. partially submerged with liquid.
   c. steamed with aromatic vegetables and herbs.
   d. submerged in a liquid that is kept at a constant, moderate temperature.
   e. none of the above.
2. If a poached or simmered item is to be served cold, which of the following ways should it be prepared?
   a. Cooked well done.
   b. Slightly undercooked.
   c. Seared on the outside first.
   d. Shocked in ice water right away.
   e. Poached or simmered foods are never served cold.
3. Items to be steamed should be naturally tender and
   a. of a size or shape that will allow them to cook in a short amount of time.
   b. seared to form a seal on the outside, to prevent moisture and flavor loss during cooking.
   c. during cooking the lid should be taken off occasionally to allow excess steam to escape, thereby keeping the food tender.
   d. allowed to rest 10–15 minutes before serving for the juices to redistribute in the food item.
   e. all of the above.
4. Foods that have been properly prepared en papillote will demonstrate the same characteristics of flavor, appearance, and texture as
   a. shallow-poached foods.
   b. boiled foods.
   c. simmered foods.
   d. poached foods.
   e. none of the above.
5. Boiled foods are actually cooked by what technique?
   a. Steaming.
   b. Simmering.
   c. Poaching.
   d. Shallow poaching.
   e. En papillote.

True/False

1. _____ When poaching or simmering, a pot that is too large will not produce a flavorful product because the amount of liquid needed to cover the product will be greater.

2. _____ Covering a pot when cooking has the effect of creating pressure, which allows the liquid's temperature to become lower.

3. _____ Unlike dry-heat methods, moist-heat cookery does not form a seal on the food as an initial step in the cooking process.

4. _____ When cooking food items en papillote, the steam created by the foods natural juices cooks the food.

5. _____ In shallow poaching, no significant flavor is transferred between the food and the poaching liquid.

Fill in the Blank

1. _____ generally contain a greater proportion of nutrients because water-soluble nutrients are not drawn out of the food as readily.

2. When cooking food items en papillote, the main item rests on a bed of herbs, vegetables, or sauce, and the combination of these ingredients and the natural juices serves _____.

3. Like sautéing and grilling, shallow poaching is an _____ technique suited to foods that are cut into portion size or smaller pieces.

4. Poaching and simmering are techniques that call for a food to be completely submerged in a liquid that is kept at a _____ temperature.

5. With the exception of _____, all moist-heat methods of cooking require the use of naturally tender meat, poultry, or fish.

Discussion

1. What is the fundamental difference between moist- and dry-heat cooking?
2. Why is it advisable to wrap or coat food that is to be steamed?
3. Why do steamed foods generally contain a greater proportion of nutrients?
4. What types of food are best suited for steaming?
5. Explain some possible types of liquids that can be used for steaming foods.
6. How do you determine doneness in steamed foods?
7. Briefly describe the three factors used to evaluate quality in steamed foods.
8. Briefly describe the method for steaming food.
9. What is the basic concept of cooking foods en papillote?
10. In regard to cooking en papillote, what prepreparation can be done to thicker cuts of meat and vegetables to insure that they are properly cooked?
11. What are some of the difficulties in determining doneness with foods cooked en papillote?
12. What three factors are used when evaluating quality with foods cooked en papillote?
13. Briefly describe the procedure for cooking a food item en papillote.
14. Shallow poaching is a combination of what two techniques?
15. When shallow poaching, why is the poaching liquid often used as part of the sauce?
16. Why is shallow poaching an à la minute technique?
17. What are some of the methods to finish cooking shallow-poached food items?
18. How do you determine doneness in shallow-poached foods?
19. Briefly describe the three factors used in evaluating quality in shallow-poached foods.
20. What would deposits of white albumin on fish signify if it were shallow poached?
21. Briefly describe the method for shallow poaching a food item.
22. When poaching and simmering, what distinction is made between them to tell them apart?
23. What is the difference in the types of foods used in poaching and simmering?
24. Why are simmered foods often referred to as "boiled"?
25. Why are very few foods truly boiled?
26. Briefly discuss the types of liquids that can be used to poach and simmer food items.
27. When simmering or poaching, why do you bring the liquid to a simmer before adding the food item?
28. Why is it important to choose the correct size pot when simmering or poaching?
29. Why is it important to have the food item completely submerged when poaching or simmering?
30. What effect does covering a pot have in relation to its temperature?
31. How is doneness determined in simmered and poached food items?
32. What should be done to simmered or poached foods that are to be served chilled?
33. What three factors are used to evaluate quality in poached or simmered foods?
34. Briefly describe the method for poaching and simmering.

What Went Wrong?

1. A "Boiled New England Dinner" is featured on the menu. But on one particular evening, the vegetables appear gray and the meat is tough and stringy.
2. The steamed snapper with a sake sauce seems bland, and the flesh of the snapper is almost dry.

Chapter *21*

Combination Cooking Methods

This chapter introduces and describes the combination methods, so known because more than one type of cooking method is used to produce a completed dish. The most commonly used techniques require a combination of dry heat (searing the main item) and moist heat (simmering in a flavorful liquid once the initial searing is completed). There are many optional steps used to produce special results. The student will learn many of these variations through reading and preparing specific recipes. The basic principles will remain the same.

After reading and studying this chapter, you should be able to:

1. Explain why stewing and braising are considered "combination methods."
2. Explain and use the basic procedure for braising.
3. Explain and use the basic procedure for stewing, including the procedure for preparing a "white stew."
4. Identify the various foods that are suitable for these combination techniques.
5. Properly determine doneness and evaluate the quality of braised and stewed items.
6. Identify other recipes that make use of a combination of techniques that are based on braising and stewing.

Matching

1. _____ Blanquette

2. _____ Pot roast

3. _____ Swissing

4. _____ Goulash

5. _____ Daube

6. _____ Braising

a. A white stew traditionally made from white meat or lamb, and garnished with mushrooms and pearl onions.

b. A stew traditionally prepared with lamb or mutton and root vegetables, onions, and peas.

c. A common American term for braising, and the name of a traditional dish.

d. A general term used to describe food that is first seared and then cooked slowly in a liquid medium.

e. A Mediterranean-style fish stew, combining a variety of fish and shellfish.

f. A French term for stew, this literally translates as "restores the appetite."

7. _____ Estouffade

g. Braising technique often associated with portion-sized meats that are repeatedly dredged in flour and pounded.

8. _____ Stewing

h. A braise customarily made from red meats that includes red wine. The name is a variation of the type of cooking vessel it is prepare in.

9. _____ Bouillabaisse

i. A special type of fish stew, typically prepared with eel.

10. _____ Ragout

j. A white stew often made with veal, poultry, or small game.

11. _____ Fricassée

k. A French term used for the braising method and the dish itself.

12. _____ Matelote

l. A stew originated in Hungary, seasoned and colored with paprika and served with dumplings and potatoes.

13. _____ Navarin

m. A technique similar to braising, where the main item is cut into bite-size pieces.

Multiple Choice

1. In stewing, the amount of liquid used in relation to the amount of item
   a. is always less than braising.
   b. is about the same as braising.
   c. varies from one style of preparation to another.
   d. is more than braising.
   e. none of the above.
2. Tender food items can be braised or stewed, but require
   a. less cooking liquid.
   b. a lower temperature.
   c. a shorter cooking time.
   d. all of the above.
   e. none of the above.
3. The basic difference between braising and stewing is that
   a. braising is always done on top of the stove and stewing is done in the oven.
   b. in stewing, the main item is cut into small, bite-size pieces.
   c. braised foods are seared, whereas stewed foods are blanched.
   d. stewed food items are always made from fish or game and braised items are made from red meats only.
   e. all of the above.
4. The first step for most braises is to
   a. sear the main item in a small amount of hot fat.
   b. blanch the main item in salted water.
   c. sweat or caramelize the mirepoix.
   d. cut the meat into bite-size portions.
   e. any of the above, depending on what type of braised item you are preparing.
5. Dredging a main item in flour before braising will
   a. help the meat to caramelize.
   b. help retain the juices inside the meat.
   c. help to thicken the sauce during cooking.
   d. eliminate the need for trussing.
   e. none of the above.

True/False

1. _____ In braising, relatively little liquid is used in relation to the main item's volume.

2. _____ Tomatoes, frequently used in braised dishes, act as a tenderizer to break down the tough tissues of less tender meats and give the finished dish additional flavor and color.

3. _____ When stewing, searing the meat will assist in developing moisture and texture.

4. _____ Braising in the oven tends to result in a inferior product that lends itself to scorching easily.

5. _____ The essential components for stews are the same as for braising; however, the proportion of liquid to main product changes slightly.

Fill in the Blank

1. When preparing a stew, blanching improves the _____ and _____ of the finished product.

2. Preparations that are braised or stewed traditionally have a robust flavor and are often thought of as _____.

3. Foods to be braised are traditionally _____, _____, and _____ than foods prepared by dry-heat and moist-heat techniques.

4. When braising, mirepoix furnishes both _____ and _____. It also elevates the main item somewhat from the pot bottom and helps to prevent it from sticking.

5. Some stews call for only a small amount of liquid, relying on the main item's natural juices to provide moisture. This is especially true for stews made from naturally tender foods, such as _____ and _____.

Discussion

1. What types of foods are considered appropriate for combination cooking methods?
2. What general guidelines are used when braising or simmering more tender food items?
3. In braising, what is the first step in preparation?
4. What can be said about the size of food items that are to be braised? How much liquid can be used with braised food items?
5. What are two benefits of braising?
6. What purpose does searing provide when braising?
7. Why does braising in the oven result in a better product?
8. What precautions should be taken if braising is done on the stove-top?
9. What types of foods are traditionally used for braising?
10. Briefly discuss some optional components that can be used with braising.
11. When braising, what is the difference in technique when searing red and white meats and seafood?
12. What three purposes does a mirepoix serve in braising?
13. What is the purpose of removing the lid during the final portion of the cooking time when braising?
14. What is the purpose of reducing the braising liquid when the item has completed cooking?
15. What options do you have with the mirepoix when braising?
16. How do you determine doneness with braising food items?
17. What three factors are used when evaluating the quality for braised food items?
18. Briefly describe the procedure for braising.
19. Although stewing is similar to braising, what is the main difference between the two?
20. What can be said about the amount of liquid to be used with a stewed food item?
21. Why is the cooking time for stews generally shorter than that for braised foods?
22. What can be said for the essential ingredients in stews in relation to braising?
23. Besides searing, what can be done to meat to be stewed in order to improve its flavor and color?

24. How do you determine doneness with stews?
25. What three factors are used when evaluating quality for stews?
26. In braising and stewing, what accounts for the sauce's exceptional body?
27. Why does the text point out that contemporary renditions of classic dishes, such as a navarin, can be made with lobster instead of mutton?

What Went Wrong?

The Yankee pot roast does not seem to have as full a flavor as usual, the meat is tough and hard to chew, and the sauce seems watery.

Chapter 22

Vegetable Cookery

Vegetable cookery has experienced a dramatic increase in importance, as several factors have influenced the way Americans are eating. This chapter teaches the proper methods for "prepping" vegetables, using a variety of cooking techniques, organized in the same general categories as meat cookery. After reading and studying this chapter, you should be able to:

1. Explain and understand the basic guidelines of vegetable cookery, including purchasing, handling, and preliminary preparation techniques.
2. Evaluate cooking methods in terms of how they will affect the overall quality of the vegetable—nutrient and color retention, flavor, and texture.
3. Determine the correct degree of doneness for different vegetables, based on type of vegetable, the cooking method used, and regional and cultural differences.
4. Use proper holding and reheating techniques.
5. Properly cook vegetables by moist-heat methods: boiling, steaming, pan-steaming, and cooking in the microwave.
6. Properly cook vegetables by dry-heat methods: sautéing, panfrying, baking/roasting, grilling, and broiling.
7. Properly cook vegetables by combination method: stewing and braising.

Matching

1. _____ Roasting/baking

2. _____ Blanching

3. _____ Pan-steaming

4. _____ Al dente

5. _____ Panfrying

6. _____ Grilling/broiling

a. Vegetables are usually blanched first, and then breaded and cooked in large amounts of fat.

b. A way of reheating vegetables without browning them. This is a way to finish vegetables in butter.

c. A term translated as "to the tooth," meaning that the food should have some texture and not be mushy.

d. A type of boiling used to remove skin, eliminate odors, or "set" colors.

e. A technique that involves a radiant heat source. The vegetables are often marinated before cooking.

f. A technique using a vapor bath. A practical and efficient method of preparing vegetables for à la minute service.

7. _____ Glazing

g. A moist-heat technique that cooks by causing the food's molecules to vibrate and cause friction.

8. _____ Parcooking/parboiling

h. A moist-heat cooking technique that is a combination of boiling and steaming.

9. _____ Microwave

i. Similar to sautéing, but the amount of cooking medium is increased. The vegetables used in this preparation are sometimes breaded.

10. _____ Sautéing/stir-frying

j. Cooking techniques that use the combination methods of preparation.

11. _____ Stewing and braising

k. A dry heat technique best suited for thick-skinned vegetables that may otherwise be tough to peel.

12. _____ Deep-frying

l. A technique used to partially cook vegetables to be used in other preparations, such as braises, grilles, or gratins.

13. _____ Steaming

m. To coat vegetables with liquefied sugar or sugar syrups.

Multiple Choice

1. Microwaving is essentially what type of cooking method?
   a. Radiant.
   b. Dry heat.
   c. Moist heat.
   d. Roasting/baking.
   e. None of the above.
2. In order to correctly determine doneness, a chef should be able to understand
   a. the characteristics of the vegetable when properly cooked.
   b. the normal standard of quality for a particular cooking technique.
   c. regional or cultural preferences regarding doneness.
   d. the natural characteristics of the vegetable.
   e. all of the above.
3. Generally speaking, the best color is retained when vegetables
   a. have salt added to the water.
   b. are started in cold water and gradually brought to a boil.
   c. are cooked for as short a time as possible.
   d. are allowed to soak in water ahead of time.
   e. all of the above.
4. In contemporary menu planning, the primary importance of vegetables is to
   a. add visual and textural interest.
   b. round out and balance a meal's nutritional content.
   c. "fill up" the a plate.
   d. pair a cooking technique with a particular vegetable with which it is not ordinarily associated.
   e. all of the above.
5. Vegetable stews and braises are excellent ways to retain vitamins and minerals lost form the vegetable into the cooking liquid because
   a. the liquid is served as part of the dish.
   b. a beurre manié or arrowroot is added to seal in the vitamins and minerals.
   c. braises and stews are in fact low in vitamins and minerals and should be avoided whenever possible in contemporary menus.
   d. they are never peeled, trimmed, or blanched, and this acts to retain the vitamins and minerals.
   e. none of the above.

True/False

1. _____ The distinction between a vegetable stew and braise is the same as for meats: The vegetables in a stew are customarily cut into small pieces, whereas those in a braise are cut in large pieces or are left whole.

2. _____ Denser green vegetables, such as broccoli, should be boiled, covered, to allow the natural acid to retain the vegetable's color.

3. _____ When reheating vegetables in the microwave, use the lowest setting on the microwave and reheat them gently and slowly.

4. _____ When sautéing vegetables, as with sautéing meats, it is important to brown the exterior of the vegetable.

5. _____ Chili peppers hold most of their heat in the seeds and ribs.

Fill in the Blank

1. Ideally, the _____ should serve as the chef's guide in choosing what vegetables to purchase in any given season.

2. _____ or _____ vegetables, unlike most vegetables, will withstand being held in stainless-steel bain-maries or loosely covered hotel pans, in a steam table.

3. The change in flavor, during cooking, of any vegetable will depend both on the _____ and the _____ used.

4. Roasting or baking is best suited to vegetables that have _____ that will protect the interior from drying or scorching.

5. When finishing a hot puréed vegetable, the vegetable and heavy cream or other liquids should be at the _____; butter should be _____ but not melted.

Discussion

1. Why are vegetables important in contemporary menu planning?
2. Briefly describe some examples on how different vegetable cooking methods produce specific and characteristic results.
3. What is one way to broaden the repertoire of vegetable dishes?
4. What is the best overall way to assure quality when cooking vegetables?
5. Briefly explain why the market should be the chef's guide when purchasing vegetables.
6. Why should vegetables be "prepped" as close to service as possible?
7. Briefly describe the procedure for cleaning leeks.
8. Why is it important to "string" peas and beans?
9. What are the two areas of concern when preparing artichokes?
10. What is the purpose of cooking vegetables?
11. In order to determine doneness, what must the chef understand?
12. When determining doneness, what two tests are used, bearing in mind the style of cookery, the vegetable itself, and the desired result?
13. What should you avoid when holding heated vegetables for service?
14. What are three methods of properly reheating vegetables for service?
15. Generally speaking, what is the best way to retain colors in vegetables?
16. What are five ways to minimize loss of nutrients when cooking vegetables?
17. What will affect the flavor retention of vegetables during cooking?
18. Regarding cooking techniques in general, what three guidelines should be followed?
19. What is the difference between blanching and parcooking or parboiling?
20. What various liquids can be used to boil vegetables?
21. Briefly describe the method for boiling vegetables.

22. Why is steaming a very good technique for cooking vegetables?
23. Why is it important to steam vegetables in a single layer?
24. Briefly describe the method for steaming and pan-steaming.
25. Briefly describe the cooking process that takes place when vegetables are microwaved.
26. What two ways can vegetables be cooked in a microwave. Why would you choose one method over another?
27. Briefly describe the method for microwaving vegetables. What should the power setting be when cooking?
28. What types of vegetables are best suited for roasting/baking?
29. What should the texture of vegetables be that have been roasted/baked?
30. What optional components can be used when roasting/baking vegetables?
31. How can vegetables be "prepped" for roasting/baking?
32. Why are some vegetables sautéed from their raw state, while others are partially cooked?
33. Describe the term "finishing in butter."
34. What is glazing, and what ingredients are used? Also, give the method.
35. What is the difference in sautéing vegetables and red meats?
36. How can vegetables be "prepped" for panfrying?
37. Why are few vegetables deep-fried from their raw state?
38. What type of batter is often used to coat deep-fried vegetables?
39. Briefly describe the procedure for deep-frying vegetables.
40. What types of vegetables lend themselves to grilling/broiling?
41. What are some differences and similarities with grilling and broiling vegetables?
42. Briefly describe the procedure for grilling and broiling vegetables.
43. What distinction is made between braised and stewed vegetables?
44. Briefly describe the method for stewing and braising vegetables.
45. How are puréed vegetables served?
46. Briefly describe the method for puréeing vegetables.

What Went Wrong?

1. A vegetable for the evening's service has a poor color and seems undercooked, with a strong, unpleasant flavor.
2. The red cabbage has turned blue.
3. The broccoli is brilliantly green and completely soft.

Chapter 23

Potato Cookery

This chapter focuses on the correct procedure for preparing potatoes (including sweet potatoes) by a number of different techniques. After reading and studying this chapter, you should be able to:

1. Identify a variety of potatoes and describe them in terms of their characteristics when cooked.
2. Properly cook potatoes by moist heat methods: boiling and steaming.
3. Properly cook potatoes using dry heat: baking/roasting and en casserole.
4. Properly cook potatoes in fat: sautéing/panfrying and deep-frying.
5. Properly prepare a purée and a number of items based on purées.

Matching

1. _____ Blanching

2. _____ Lorette potatoes

3. _____ New potatoes

4. _____ Solanine

5. _____ Multi-stage technique

6. _____ Duchesse potatoes

7. _____ Idaho/russet

8. _____ Roësti potatoes

9. _____ Single-stage technique

a. A process where a potato undergoes one or more preliminary techniques before it becomes a finished dish.

b. An all-purpose potato that has a moderate amount of moisture and starch.

c. An example of a deep-fried potato purée.

d. A toxin present in the skin of the potato. Its presence is detected by its green color.

e. In this procedure, the potato is taken from the raw state to the finished state, using a single cooking technique.

f. An example of a potato cooked using the sautéing/panfrying technique.

g. A term that applies to any potato harvested when quite small. These potatoes are high in moisture and sugar and low in starch.

h. A technique where the potato is peeled, combined with heavy cream, a sauce, or uncooked custard, and slowly baked until it is extremely tender.

i. A process done to many deep-fried potatoes that insures that they will have the proper color, texture, and flavor and be properly cooked, but not greasy or scorched.

10. _____ Chef's potatoes

11. _____ En casserole

12. _____ Dauphinoise potatoes

j. An example of potatoes that are cooked "en casserole."

k. An example of a potato dish that is prepared by the puréeing method.

l. A type of potato that is high in starch and low in moisture. Also known as "bakers."

Multiple Choice

1. A potato that is to be puréed must first be
   a. steamed.
   b. baked.
   c. boiled.
   d. any of the above.
   e. steamed or boiled only.
2. In order for potatoes to retain most of their nutrients, they should be
   a. cooked in their skins if possible.
   b. blanched to "set" the vitamins in the potato.
   c. cooked using only multi-stage techniques.
   d. cooked using only single-stage techniques.
   e. none of the above.
3. A variation of roasting/baking potatoes that calls for a parcooked potato to be browned and glazed with the released drippings from a roast is called
   a. roësti potatoes.
   b. oven-roasting.
   c. en casserole.
   d. potatoes au gratin.
   e. potatoes Anna.
4. In relation to cooking potatoes, sautéing and panfrying terms can be used interchangeably because
   a. they use the same amount of fat.
   b. the same types of fats are always used.
   c. there is no difference in the end product.
   d. chef's potatoes are used for both techniques.
   e. none of the above.
5. Which types of the following potato dishes is particularly suitable for banquet service because they are easy to divide into portions and serve, and can be held briefly without loss of quality?
   a. Boiled or steamed.
   b. Panfried/sautéed.
   c. Deep-fried.
   d. En casserole.
   e. All of the above.

True/False

1. _____ Potatoes can be shocked in cold water to stop the cooking process.

2. _____ Idaho or russet potatoes, also known as "bakers," are naturally low in starch and high in moisture.

3. _____ Potatoes that are to be puréed are often steamed because this technique produces a more moist product than does boiling.

4. _____ Wrapping potatoes to be baked in aluminum will insure that the potato skin will become crisp during cooking.

5. _____ Potatoes that are to be deep-fried for such preparations as straw or matchstick potatoes should not be rinsed so that they won't clump together as they cook.

Fill in the Blank

1. When deep-frying, _____ potatoes are preferred because of their _____ starch and _____ moisture content.
2. _____ and _____, though not botanically related to the potato, share several characteristics with it and can be treated in the same manner.
3. When cooking new potatoes, their naturally sweet flavor is most enhanced when they are prepared by _____ or _____.
4. When preparing potatoes en casserole, a very creamy texture can be achieved by preparing the dish in a _____; this will also prevent a custard from curdling.
5. The higher the starch content in a potato, the more _____ and _____ it will be after it is cooked.

Discussion

1. Why are sweet potatoes and yams cooked with the same methods as potatoes?
2. What are the general characteristics of russet, chef's, and new potatoes? What types of cooking methods lend themselves to each variety and why?
3. What does a green color on the skin of a potato indicate? What must be done to a potato that has this green color?
4. What is the advantage of cooking potatoes in their skins?
5. If you store peeled potatoes in water, why is it a good idea to cook the potatoes in that same water?
6. What is the single-stage cooking technique for potatoes? Give a few examples of potato preparations that use this technique.
7. What is the multi-stage cooking technique for potatoes? Give a few examples of potato preparations that use this technique.
8. Give the procedure for preparing boiled potatoes.
9. When are boiled potatoes properly dried?
10. What is the procedure for holding boiled potatoes?
11. When preparing potatoes for puréeing, why is best to steam them?
12. What can be done to the steaming liquid to impart different flavors to the potatoes?
13. Briefly describe the procedure for steaming potatoes.
14. What are the guidelines for determining doneness, evaluating quality, and holding steamed potatoes?
15. What are the best potatoes for baking and roasting? Why?
16. What is "oven-roasting"?
17. How should potatoes be "prepped" for baking?
18. Why do you not cover potatoes with foil before baking?
19. Give the method for baking or roasting a potato.
20. What are the guidelines for determining doneness, evaluating quality, and holding baked or roasted potatoes?
21. Give the mise en place and the method for potatoes cooked "en casserole."
22. Give the guidelines for determining doneness, evaluating quality, and holding potatoes cooked "en casserole."
23. Why are potatoes cooked "en casserole" well-suited for banquet service?
24. What are the best types of potatoes to use for sautéing or panfrying? Why are these the best types to use?
25. What variety of cooking fats can be used to sauté?
26. Briefly describe the method for sautéing potatoes.
27. Give the guidelines for determining doneness, evaluating quality, and holding sautéed potatoes.
28. Why are russet potatoes the best type to use when deep-frying?
29. Why are most deep-fat–fried potatoes prepared from the raw state blanched first?

30. What is the purpose of rinsing potatoes in several changes of cold water before deep-frying?
31. What type of oil is best suited for deep-frying potatoes?
32. Briefly describe the procedure for deep-frying potatoes.
33. What are the guidelines for determining doneness, evaluating quality, and holding deep-fried potatoes?
34. How are potatoes prepared before they are puréed?
35. Why should you not use a food processor or blender when puréeing potatoes?
36. How would you prepare whipped potatoes if you were making large quantities?
37. What is the result in overworking puréed potatoes?
38. Briefly describe the procedure for puréeing potatoes.
39. Give the guidelines for determining doneness, evaluating quality, and holding puréed potatoes.
40. Briefly describe the method for deep-fry puréed potato preparations.

What Went Wrong?

1. The potato purée is lumpy, heavy, and a little gray.
2. The french fries are coming out very dark, but not properly cooked.
3. The baked potatoes at the beginning of service are delicious, fresh, and earthy tasting, but by the end of the night the skins are soft and flabby and the flesh has a slightly sweet taste.

Chapter 24

Cooking Grains and Legumes

In this chapter, the student will learn the proper methods of preparing a variety of whole grains, meal, and dried legumes, as well as general guidelines for storing. After reading and studying this chapter, you should be able to:

1. Identify a variety of whole grains and also give general guidelines for storage and advance preparation, where appropriate.
2. Identify a variety of legumes and give general guidelines for storage.
3. Use both long- and short-soak methods to soften legumes before cooking.
4. Prepare legumes and grains by boiling and properly determine doneness.
5. Prepare couscous by steaming.
6. Prepare grains by the pilaf method.
7. Prepare risotto.

Matching

1. _____ Pilaf

   a. A combination of cornmeal, butter, water, and salt that is slowly simmered.

2. _____ Hominy

   b. A part of a grain that serves as the storage facility for carbohydrates, vitamins, minerals, and some of the proteins and oils used by the plant.

3. _____ Risotto

   c. Seeds that grow in pods that can be used fresh or dried.

4. _____ Legumes

   d. A small opening in a legume that allows water to be absorbed through the tough seed coats.

5. _____ Polenta

   e. The term referring to dried corn left whole.

6. _____ Hilum

   f. A method of cooking short-grain rice by stirring constantly as stock is added a small amount at a time and is absorbed by the grain.

7. _____ Grains

   g. A grain dish in which the grain is first heated in the pan, either dry or in oil, and then combined with hot liquid.

8. _____ Endosperm

   h. A term used to describe the fruit of a grass.

Multiple Choice

1. If adding an acidic liquid to a rice pilaf, what happens to the cooking time?
   a. It will decrease.
   b. It will increase.
   c. It will stay the same, but less salt will be needed.
   d. An acidic liquid should never be added to a pilaf.
   e. None of the above.
2. Which of the following types of short-grain rice is traditionally used for making risotto?
   a. Hominy.
   b. Arborio.
   c. Couscous.
   d. Polenta.
   e. Any of the above can be used for risotto.
3. The purpose of cooking grains and legumes is to
   a. deactivate various naturally present substances that have unpleasant or even harmful effects by either directly or indirectly causing vitamin deficiencies.
   b. change their texture enough to make them easy to chew.
   c. develop an acceptable flavor.
   d. all of the above.
   e. none of the above.
4. Soaking is not an essential in the advance preparation in grains and legumes, although it
   a. is always necessary when making a pilaf.
   b. is usually done with grains but not legumes.
   c. is helpful in shortening the cooking time.
   d. soaking is in fact an essential advance preparation.
   e. none of the above.
5. An example of one of the few grains that is actually steamed is
   a. couscous.
   b. polenta.
   c. rice pilaf.
   d. steamed rice.
   e. risotto.

True/False

1. _____ If wine is to be used when making a risotto, it should be added at the beginning of the cooking process.

2. _____ Milled grains, especially enriched, converted, and polished rices, need not be rinsed.

3. _____ Cooked legumes may be held for several days without losing quality if properly stored and reheated.

4. _____ The grains most nutrient-rich part is the hilum.

5. _____ When preparing a pilaf, heating the grain in hot fat or oil begins to gelatinize the starches. This encourages the grains to remain separate after they are cooked.

Fill in the Blank

1. Legumes will take a _____ time to cook as they become older.
2. Grains may be cooked by using _____; legumes, however, are _____.
3. Although in either method used for soaking legumes (long or short) it is not essential to change the water during or after soaking, some people believe that draining legumes results in a more _____ product.
4. The best risotto has an almost porridge-like consistency, with each grain retaining a _____.
5. Grains are often cooked in an amount of liquid that is _____ than they can actually absorb.

Discussion

1. What are grains? Discuss some of the milling processes used in the production of grains.
2. What is the endosperm? What is its significance?
3. What are legumes, and in what forms can they be purchased?
4. What are the advantages of combining grain and legumes in one's diet?
5. What are the three purposes of cooking grains and legumes?
6. What are the proper storage techniques for grains and legumes?
7. What is the importance of sorting and rinsing grains and legumes?
8. What types of grains should not be rinsed and why?
9. What is the purpose of soaking grains and legumes?
10. What is a hilum, and what is its significance when soaking grains and legumes?
11. List and describe the two techniques used to soak legumes and grains.
12. Give the guidelines for holding grains and legumes after they have been cooked.
13. Briefly describe the procedure for boiling grains and legumes.
14. What effect do acidic ingredients have during the cooking process of grains and legumes?
15. Briefly describe the guidelines for determining doneness and evaluating quality in grains and legumes that have been boiled.
16. What types of grains are usually used for steaming?
17. What is a couscoussière, and how is it used?
18. Briefly describe the procedure for steaming grains.
19. How may some grains be "prepped" before steaming?
20. What are the guidelines for determining doneness and evaluating quality for steamed grains?
21. What is a general definition of a pilaf?
22. What types of cooking liquids can be used with a pilaf?
23. What will the effect of adding an acidic liquid have on cooking a pilaf?
24. When making a pilaf, what effect does heating the grain in hot oil or fat have on the final product?
25. Briefly describe the procedure for preparing a rice pilaf.
26. What are the guidelines for determining doneness and evaluating quality with rice pilafs?
27. What type of rice is customarily used for risotto?
28. What accounts for a risotto's creamy texture when properly cooked?
29. Briefly describe some of the ingredients traditionally used in risotto.
30. If using wine in a risotto, when is the best time to add it?
31. Briefly describe the method for preparing a risotto.
32. What advance preparation can be done to risotto in order to serve it throughout a service period without losing quality?
33. What are the guidelines for determining doneness and evaluating quality in a risotto?
34. What are some advantages of using grains and legumes on contemporary menus?

What Went Wrong?

1. The rice pilaf is sticky and pasty-tasting.
2. The risotto is not creamy.
3. The beans are crunchy, even after they have simmered for 3 hours.

Chapter 25

Cooking Pasta and Dumplings

This chapter is devoted to the correct procedure for preparing a wide variety of pastas, including fresh pasta and dumplings. It also instructs the reader in the correct method for cooking pastas, once prepared. After reading and studying this chapter, you should be able to:

1. Prepare fresh pasta dough by hand, in a food processor and in a mixer.
2. Roll out fresh pasta dough, using a rolling pin and a sheeting pasta machine.
3. Use the ratio for fresh pasta variations in order to make pastas with special colors and flavors.
4. Cut pasta, using a pasta machine or a knife.
5. Prepare a variety of dumplings, including gnocchi and spatzli.

Matching

1. _____ Spatzli

2. _____ Ziti and macaroni

3. _____ Semolina

4. _____ Pasta

5. _____ Dim sum

6. _____ Fettucine and linguine

7. _____ Gnocchi

8. _____ Al dente

9. _____ Dumpling

a. A term used to describe the proper stage to cook pasta. Literally means "to the tooth" in Italian.

b. A dumpling made from a pourable batter.

c. Examples of long, flat pastas.

d. An example of a dumpling that is used in Italian cooking.

e. Examples of tube-shaped pastas.

f. A very broad category of doughs and batters, ranging from bread to puréed potatoes.

g. Coarsely ground, hard wheat endosperm used for pastas and dumplings.

h. A mixture of flour, eggs, and salt, kneaded and cut into various shapes.

i. A term used to describe a category of assorted Chinese dumplings.

Multiple Choice

1. Dried pastas are usually served
   a. with light butter or cream sauces.
   b. cold with a vinaigrette sauce.
   c. generally with no sauce at all.
   d. with heartier sauces that, such as those that contain meat.
   e. none of the above.

2. Pasta and dumplings are prepared from a dough or batter that always includes
   a. flour.
   b. a starchy ingredient.
   c. potatoes.
   d. meal.
   e. none of the above.

3. Oil made be added to some pastas to
   a. extend its shelf life.
   b. help the dough adhere better during cutting and filling.
   c. provide richness and color.
   d. keep the dough from oxidizing when exposed to air.
   e. all of the above.

4. When cooking any pasta, the ratio of water to pasta should be
   a. 2:1.
   b. 4:1.
   c. 6:1.
   d. 8:1.
   e. 10:1.

5. The cooking time for dried pasta in relation to fresh pasta
   a. is longer.
   b. is always shorter.
   c. is about the same.
   d. doesn't matter if the water is at a full boil.
   e. none of the above.

True/False

1. _____ To hold pasta once it has been cooked, rinse it thoroughly with cold water and toss it in a small amount of oil to keep the strands from clumping together.

2. _____ Many dumplings are initially poached and finished in a variety of ways.

3. _____ When making fresh pasta, to ensure proper texture, some all-purpose white flour may need to be incorporated.

4. _____ In general, freshly made pasta should be smooth, fairly elastic, and slightly dry to the touch.

5. _____ Dried pasta can be held in dry storage almost indefinitely.

Fill in the Blank

1. When making fresh pasta, if the ingredients contain high moisture levels, it may be necessary to adjust the basic formula by using _____ or _____.

2. The three basic ways to mix pasta dough are _____, _____, or _____.

3. When making fresh pasta, the _____ is particularly important if the dough is to be rolled by hand; if the dough is not sufficiently _____, it will be difficult to roll into thin sheets.

4. The delicate flavor of fresh pasta is most successfully paired with a _____ or _____ sauce.
5. Eggs are frequently included in fresh pasta to provide _____ and _____.

Discussion

1. What are some differences between a pasta dough and a batter?
2. What are three differences between dried and fresh pasta?
3. What types of flours can be used to make fresh pasta?
4. What are the functions of eggs and oil in a pasta dough?
5. If other seasonings are added to fresh pasta, what precautions should be taken with those ingredients?
6. How should saffron be added to pasta dough?
7. What are the three methods for mixing pasta dough?
8. Briefly describe each procedure for mixing pasta dough.
9. What is the purpose of "resting" pasta dough before it is rolled into sheets?
10. What are the guidelines for evaluating quality with mixed pasta dough?
11. Briefly describe the procedure for rolling pasta dough with a machine.
12. Briefly describe the procedure for rolling pasta dough by hand.
13. What is the purpose of drying pasta before it is cut into a specific shape?
14. What is the procedure for holding fresh pasta before cooking?
15. When cooking pasta, what is the ratio of water to pasta?
16. What are some differences between cooking fresh and dried pastas?
17. How do you hold cooked pasta if it is to be held chilled?
18. Briefly describe the guidelines for determining doneness and evaluating quality for dried and fresh pastas.
19. What are some of the guidelines for pairing sauces with various shapes of pastas?
20. Briefly describe the procedures for serving pastas for a la carte, banquet, and buffet service.
21. Briefly describe the procedure for cooking pastas.
22. What does the term "dumpling" mean?
23. What are some of the ways that dumpling can be prepared?
24. Briefly describe the three methods for shaping spatzli.
25. Briefly describe the guidelines for determining doneness and evaluating quality when preparing dumplings.
26. Briefly describe the holding and serving techniques for dumplings.

What Went Wrong?

1. The pasta sticks together and cannot be served.
2. The dumplings served with chicken stew are tough and heavy.

Chapter 26

Breakfast and Egg Cookery

This category of cooking is often referred to as "pantry cooking." It encompasses a broad range of preparations and techniques that have applications well beyond service at breakfast. After reading and studying this chapter, you should be able to:

1. Prepare eggs in a variety of methods, including cooked in the shell, baked, poached, fired, scrambled, omelets, and quiches.
2. Prepare savory and sweet soufflés.
3. Prepare a variety of breakfast items based on batters, including pancakes, crêpes, waffles, and French toast.
4. Prepare breakfast meats, including hash, sausages, bacon, and ham.
5. Prepare coffee, tea, and other breakfast beverages.

Matching

1. _____ Rolled omelet

2. _____ Quiche

3. _____ Scrapple

4. _____ Sunny-side up eggs

5. _____ Hash

6. _____ Over-easy eggs

7. _____ Frittata

8. _____ Souffléed omelet

9. _____ Pancake

a. A chopped pan fried mixture of meats, potatoes, and onions.

b. Fried cakes, made from a batter, that can be sweet or savory.

c. A fried egg that is cooked and turned while the yolk is still runny.

d. A cross between cornmeal mush and sausage.

e. An omelet where the eggs may be separated and whipped, producing a very light "fluffy" omelet.

f. Beaten egg whips added to a base. The base may take on many forms and be seasoned, depending on its name.

g. A custard baked in a crust.

h. A mixture of grains, nuts, dried fruits, coconut, and a sweetener.

i. A fried egg cooked so that the white is cooked through and the yolk is soft and runny. The egg is not turned or flipped during the cooking process.

10. _____ Granola

11. _____ Soufflé

j. French-style omelet.

k. A flat omelet, also known as a "farmer's" omelet.

Multiple Choice

1. Cooling and peeling hard-boiled eggs immediately after they have finished cooking will prevent
   a. the eggs from spoiling too soon.
   b. the shells from cracking.
   c. a green ring from forming around the yolk.
   d. the eggs from becoming "water logged."
   e. all of the above.

2. Vinegar is added to the water when poaching eggs
   a. to prevent them from getting overcooked.
   b. to help prevent the egg whites from spreading.
   c. to prevent a green ring from forming around the yolk.
   d. only to season them.
   e. none of the above.

3. Among the most nutritious offerings on a breakfast menu are
   a. fried eggs and ham.
   b. cereals.
   c. waffles and pancakes.
   d. hash and scrapple.
   e. none of the above.

4. When preparing eggs in the shell, the cooking times are measured
   a. when the egg is put in the water.
   b. when the water reaches a full boil.
   c. when the water is cold and the fire is started.
   d. when the water comes back to a simmer after the egg has been added.
   e. all of the above.

5. Brewed coffee does not hold well for more than
   a. 45 minutes to an hour.
   b. 15 to 30 minutes.
   c. 1½ to 2 hours.
   d. 3 hours.
   e. none of the above.

True/False

1. _____ Piercing the shell of the egg will keep it from cracking during cooking.

2. _____ Eggs that have been poached can be trimmed, held in cold water, and reheated in simmering water.

3. _____ For the best possible result, scrambled eggs should only be prepared to order.

4. _____ Every food service operation should be willing to grind the coffee beans before brewing each pot.

5. _____ Frittatas are also known as souffléed omelet.

Fill in the Blank

1. As water runs through the coffee, the ground coffee's flavor and essential oils _____ are into the water.
2. The process of making tea involves creating an _____.
3. When cooking an omelet, keep the pan and eggs _____ as the omelet cooks.
4. In general, if a pancake batter contains baking powder or beaten egg whites, it must be _____.
5. Hard-boiled eggs are more frequently begun in _____.

Discussion

1. Discuss some different ways that "boiled eggs" are prepared and used.
2. Briefly discuss some of the myths and facts about hard-boiled eggs.
3. Briefly describe the procedure for baked eggs.
4. What is the advantages of using very fresh eggs when poaching.
5. Briefly describe the procedure for poaching eggs.
6. How can poached eggs be handled for advance preparation?
7. Describe the doneness for the following fried eggs:
    a. Sunny-side up.
    b. Over easy.
    c. Over medium.
    d. Over hard.
8. Briefly describe the procedure for scrambled eggs.
9. List and describe the three basic types of omelets.
10. Briefly describe the procedure for preparing a rolled omelet.
11. Briefly describe the procedure for preparing a flat omelet.
12. Briefly describe the procedure for preparing a souffléed omelet.
13. What is the basic ratio of ingredients in a quiche custard?
14. What are the basic components of a soufflé?
15. What tends to be the "trickiest" part in preparing a soufflé?
16. Briefly describe the procedure for preparing dessert and savory soufflés.
17. What is the difference between pancakes, crêpes, waffles, and French toast?
18. How do you check for doneness in pancakes, crêpes, waffles, and French toast?
19. Discuss the variety of cereals, hot and cold, that can be served on a breakfast menu.
20. What are the best ways to properly cook bacon?
21. Describe a variety of ways that sausage and ham can be served for breakfast.
22. What is the traditional way to accompany hash?
23. Discuss how the following items fit into a contemporary breakfast menu:
    a. Fish.
    b. Potatoes.
    c. Fruits.
    d. Breads.
24. What is coffee, and how is it made?
25. Why should the area of coffee be of great concern to chefs?
26. How should coffee be selected for a particular establishment?
27. What is the best method for preparing tea?

What Went Wrong?

1. The hard-cooked eggs are hard to peel and have an unattractive green ring around the yolk.
2. The poached eggs are raggedy, and, of the 50 that were poached, nearly half cannot be used because the yolk broke.
3. The scrambled eggs on the buffet line are unappealing, watery, and a bright brassy color.

Chapter 27

Hors d'Oeuvre, Appetizers, and Salads

This chapter looks at the courses that are frequently the very first impression that the guest has of the chef's abilities. Offering a good selection of dishes in many categories is important, but more important than the variety is the ability to apply the most exacting standards to these dishes. After reading and studying this chapter, you should be able to:

1. Understand and explain the criteria for foods to be served as appetizers, hors d'oeuvre, and salads and the guidelines for their preparation and service.
2. Define a variety of hors d'oeuvre: finger foods, crudité, canapés, tapas, antipasto, and hors d'oeuvre variés.
3. Identify the various types of caviar and how to properly present them.
4. Identify the types of service used for hot and cold hors d'oeuvre.
5. Give a number of examples of foods, drawn from other areas of the kitchen, that may be served as appetizers, and explain what modifications, if any, might be necessary.
6. Understand the selection, preparing dressing, and service of salad greens.
7. Prepare a variety of dressings, including vinaigrettes, emulsified vinaigrettes, and mayonnaise-style dressings.
8. Understand that there are no unimportant parts to any meal.

Matching

1. _____ Vinaigrette

2. _____ Malasol

3. _____ Canapé

4. _____ Tapas

5. _____ Mayonnaise

6. _____ Crudités

7. _____ Blini

8. _____ Hors d'oeuvre

a. A small, open-faced sandwich.

b. "Self-contained" food to be eaten in no more than a bite or two.

c. Very popular finger food made with chilled vegetables and served with a dip.

d. Rectangular or oval dishes used to serve cold hors d'oeuvre.

e. Traditional French service of hot and cold hors d'oeuvre served as part of a luncheon menu.

f. Best quality of caviar, made with little salt.

g. A breed of fish from which caviar is obtained.

h. The roe of beluga, sevruga, or osetra sturgeon.

9. _____ Emulsified vinaigrette

    i. A thick, pale-ivory-colored salad dressing, made from egg yolks and oil, often containing mustard.

10. _____ Ravier

    j. Hot or cold foods served separately from the meal—either before the meal or when a meal is not served.

11. _____ Sturgeon

    k. A yeast-raised buckwheat pancake, traditionally served with caviar.

12. _____ Hors d'oeuvre variés

    l. A salad dressing usually consisting of three parts oil to one part vinegar and/or citrus juices.

13. _____ Antipasto

    m. A vinaigrette that contains egg yolks to produce a thicker dressing that will not separate.

14. _____ Finger foods

    n. Spanish-style selection of hot and cold hors d'oeuvre.

15. _____ Caviar

    o. Italian-style service of hot and cold hors d'oeuvre.

Multiple Choice

1. Traditionally, what country produces the most prized caviar?
   a. Russia or Iran.
   b. The United States.
   c. Sweden or Norway.
   d. France and Belgium.
   e. None of the above.
2. The generally accepted ratio of oil to vinegar in a vinaigrette dressing is
   a. 3 parts vinegar and/or citrus juice to 1 part oil.
   b. equal parts oil and vinegar.
   c. 2 parts vinegar and/or citrus juice to 1 part oil.
   d. 3 parts oil to 1 part vinegar and/or citrus juice.
   e. none of the above.
3. The actual selection and cooking techniques used in creating hors d'oeuvre, appetizers, and salads will depend upon
   a. what foods are intended to follow.
   b. the amount of money that can be spent.
   c. the season of the year.
   d. what the chef has available.
   e. all of the above.
4. Salad greens that are ready for service should be in pieces that are easy to pick up with a fork and in general should be about the size of
   a. half of a dollar bill.
   b. a Susan B. Anthony silver dollar.
   c. a buffalo-head nickel.
   d. a John F. Kennedy silver half-dollar.
   e. any combination of the above, less than two dollars.
5. For optimum flavor, it is advisable to make salad dressings in quantities that last no longer than
   a. three hours.
   b. three days.
   c. three weeks.
   d. three months.
   e. none of the above.

True/False

1. _____ Emulsified vinaigrettes and light mayonnaises have essentially the same ratio of major ingredients as vinaigrettes.

2. _____ A traditional canapé will have a bread base, with a spread, a filling, and a garnish.

3. _____ Connoisseurs maintain that caviar should be eaten with bone or wooden spoons, because metals can adversely affect its flavor.

4. _____ Salad greens should not be soaked to remove sand or grit, because they tend to absorb water.

5. _____ Mustard is most often added to mayonnaise for flavor, not because of any effect that the mustard might have on the dressing's stability.

Fill in the Blank

1. _____, _____, and _____ are three varieties of sturgeon that produce some of the most sought after caviars.

2. A salad dressing should always be prepared with the proper ratios, to provide the correct balance between _____ and _____.

3. With few exceptions, hors d'oeuvre should not require the guest to use a _____.

4. While hors d'oeuvre are served separately from the meal, _____ are traditionally its first course.

5. _____ served with dips are among the most popular finger foods.

Discussion

1. What criteria should be used when determining what foods should be served as hors d'oeuvre, appetizers, and salads?
2. What characteristics should foods served as hors d'oeuvre have?
3. Briefly describe the following types of hors d'oeuvre:
   a. Finger foods.
   b. Crudités.
   c. Canapés.
   d. Tapas.
   e. Hors d'oeuvre varies.
   f. Antipasto.
   g. Caviar.
4. Briefly describe some typical accompaniments that are served with somewhat saltier caviars.
5. Briefly describe the following caviar terms:
   a. Sturgeon.
   b. Beluga.
   c. Osetra.
   d. Sevruga.
   e. Malasol.
   f. Blini.
6. What three points should a chef remember when serving appetizers?
7. What four conditions are changing the place that salads typically have held on menus?
8. What criteria should be used when choosing compatible salad greens?
9. Describe the procedure for cleaning and preparing salad greens.
10. What is the generally accepted ratio of dressing to greens?
11. Discuss the procedure for a la carte salad service.
12. Briefly describe the role of special salads on contemporary menus.

13. Briefly describe the application of vinaigrettes, emulsified vinaigrettes, and mayonnaise in relation to dressing salads.
14. What is the correct balance of flavors for a vinaigrette?
15. Briefly describe the characteristics of a well-made mayonnaise.
16. Give the procedure for preparing a mayonnaise sauce.
17. Give the procedure for preparing an emulsified vinaigrette.
18. Give the procedure for preparing a vinaigrette dressing.

What Went Wrong?

1. The mayonnaise keeps breaking while it is being prepared.
2. The salad dressing is always in a big pool on the plate and the greens seem wilted.

Chapter 28

Charcuterie and Garde-manger

This chapter introduces a number of different methods and techniques to prepare sausages, pâtés, terrines, and other items. The major emphasis is on forcemeat preparations, along with a discussion of their typical applications.

After reading and studying this chapter, you should be able to:

1. Explain briefly the history of charcuterie, garde-manger, and the "cold kitchen."
2. Know the basic preparation guidelines that must be strictly followed when preparing any forcemeat.
3. Identify and prepare the following forcemeats: straight, country-style, gratin, 5/4/3, and mousseline.
4. Understand the use of panada and aspic gelée.
5. Evaluate the quality of a forcemeat.
6. Understand the method of preparation for quenelles, sausages, pâté, campagne, pâté en croute, terrines, and galantines.
7. Understand how food is to be handled before and during the smoking process.
8. Understand the preparation of gravad lox and daube.

Matching

1. _____ Galantine

2. _____ Quenelles

3. _____ Gratin forcemeat

4. _____ Pâté en croute

5. _____ Forcemeat

6. _____ T.C.M.

7. _____ Mousseline

a. A forcemeat where some portion of the dominant meat is sautéed.

b. A forcemeat baked in an earthenware mold.

c. A "tinted curing mixture" used to cure meats for a forcemeat or when smoking.

d. A well-seasoned, highly gelatinous, perfectly clarified stock. Frequently strengthened with additional gelatin.

e. A cold preparation of a variety of meats, usually including tongue, head, and feet of veal and/or pork.

f. A very light forcemeat, based on white meats or fish.

g. Combines equal parts pork meat, pork fat, and dominant meat, through a process of progressive grinding and emulsification.

8. _____ Gravad lox

9. _____ Aspic gelée

10. _____ Straight forcemeat

11. _____ Brine

12. _____ Daube

13. _____ Panada

14. _____ Terrine

15. _____ Country forcemeat

16. _____ Dry cure

h. Traditionally made from game birds and tied back into their original shape.

i. A mixture or ingredient added to forcemeats to assist in forming a good emulsion.

j. A combination of dry salts, spices, and herbs.

k. Elaborate style pâté where the mold is lined with a pastry crust.

l. A rather course forcemeat made from pork fat and meat, with a percentage of liver.

m. A lean meat and fat emulsion formed when the ingredients are forced through a sieve or grinder.

n. A combination of water, salt, spices, and other seasonings.

o. A poached dumpling served as a garnish or used to test forcemeats.

p. Salmon fillets coated with a dry-cure-and-herb mixture.

Multiple Choice

1. This term refers to items made from the pig:
   a. Garde-manger.
   b. Galantine.
   c. Charcuterie.
   d. Gravad lox.
   e. All of the above.

2. Cold smoking is done within a specified temperature range:
   a. Less than 100°F.
   b. Between 100°F and 145°F.
   c. Less than 225°F.
   d. Greater than 145°F.
   e. None of the above.

3. Pork, poultry, seafood, and dairy products can begin to lose their quality and safety rapidly when they rise above
   a. 30°F.
   b. 35°F.
   c. 40°F.
   d. 45°F.
   e. none of the above.

4. A very fine textured forcemeat used for frankfurters, bockwurst, and knockwurst is called
   a. gratin.
   b. mousseline.
   c. country-style.
   d. straight.
   e. none of the above.

5. Traditionally, the mold for a pâté de campagne would be lined with
   a. plastic wrap.
   b. aspic gelée.
   c. pâté dough.
   d. slices of fatback.
   e. all of the above.

True/False

1. _____ Pâte à choux can be used as a panada for forcemeats.

2. _____ Smoked or cured sausages generally do not require additional cooking.

3. _____ Pâté en croûte is a more elaborate style of pâté, in which the mold is lined with slices of fatback.

4. _____ Curing is an optional step for items that are to be smoked.

5. _____ Although aspic adds visual appeal by giving a sheen and luster, its basic function is to protect the product from moisture loss during storage.

Fill in the Blank

1. If a forcemeat is to be a _____, it must be kept cold throughout its preparation so that the protein and fats can combine properly.
2. In a gratin forcemeat, some portion of the _____ is sautéed and cooled before it is ground.
3. If a panada is required in a forcemeat, it should compromise no more than _____ of the forcemeat's total volume, not including garnish ingredients.
4. Pork fat is traditionally used in forcemeats. However, in the case of more delicately flavored forcemeats, _____ may be more appropriate.
5. Curing salt, a special component that combines salt with _____, is often used to produce a particular effect in forcemeats.

Discussion

1. Briefly describe the history of charcuterie and garde-manger.
2. What are the two reasons for keeping everything below 40°F when preparing forcemeats?
3. Describe the technique known as progressive grinding.
4. What is a panada, and what is its function in a forcemeat.
5. How is an aspic gelée prepared, and what is its function as related to forcemeats?
6. What three characteristics are evaluated when judging a forcemeat? Briefly explain each point.
7. Briefly explain the characteristics of the following forcemeats:
   a. Straight.
   b. Country-style.
   c. Gratin.
   d. 5/4/3.
   e. Mousseline.
8. Briefly describe the method for a straight forcemeat.
9. Briefly describe the method for a country-style forcemeat.
10. Briefly describe the method for a 5/4/3 forcemeat.
11. Briefly describe the method for a gratin forcemeat.
12. Briefly describe the method for a mousseline forcemeat.
13. What is a quenelle and describe three of its uses.
14. Discuss a variety of ways that sausages can be cooked.
15. What is the difference between a pâté de campagne and a pâté en croûte?
16. Describe the procedure for cooking a terrine.
17. Discuss the contemporary and traditional characteristics of a galantine.
18. What is the basic difference between a brine and a cure?
19. Discuss the differences between hot and cold smoking.
20. What is gravad lox, and how is it prepared?
21. What is a daube, and how is it prepared?

What Went Wrong?

1. After cooling the galantine, it is ready to be sliced, but the slices crumble.

Chapter 29

Baking Mise en Place

There are a number of special procedures, ingredients, and skills that are used in the bakeshop. This chapter is intended as a brief introduction to some of the most basic of them, including a description of the basic ingredients used in all bakeshops and the special functions they play, as well as the techniques for working with special ingredients, such as chocolate and fondant.

After reading and studying this chapter, you should be able to:
1. Name the six basic categories that ingredients usually fall into.
2. Describe some of the properties of each of these categories.
3. Identify and describe three types of leaveners.
4. Name a variety of different thickeners.
5. Explain how to properly measure (scale) ingredients, batters, and doughs.
6. Prepare baking pans properly.
7. Describe fondant, and explain how it is prepared for use.
8. Name the sequence of steps involved in tempering chocolate to use as a glaze.
9. Prepare a parchment cone and use it to make decorations.
10. Properly fill and use a pastry bag.
11. Name several pieces of equipment, pans, and other tools required in the bakeshop.

Matching

1. _____ Scaling

2. _____ Tempering

3. _____ Springform pan

4. _____ Caramelization

5. _____ Gluten

6. _____ Baking soda

7. _____ Crumb

8. _____ Baking blind

9. _____ Formula

10. _____ Fondant

a. Partially or fully baking a pie or tart crust before it is filled.

b. Term used to describe the texture of a baked item.

c. Careful measuring, using a scale.

d. A sugar and water syrup that has been cooked to a specific temperature, then worked to produce a smooth, creamy, opaque mixture used as a glaze.

e. The process of carefully melting chocolate so that it will be glossy when used as a glaze.

f. Cake pans with hinges or springs to allow the sides to be removed from the bottom.

g. Another name for a recipe used in the bakeshop.

h. An example of a chemical leavener.

i. The browning of sugar when heat is applied.

j. One of the proteins in flour that helps it give structure to baked items.

Multiple Choice

1. The reason that chocolate must be properly tempered is that
   a. it has not been completely processed by the manufacturer.
   b. it will be tasteless unless it is tempered.
   c. it has two different melting points and tempering allows the chocolate to melt smoothly and properly, without becoming grainy or streaked.
   d. it is traditional to do so.
2. Chemical leaveners do their work by
   a. creating a foam that causes the batter to rise.
   b. allowing the acids and alkalis in the batter to expand.
   c. creating a gas (carbon dioxide) when combined with the liquids present in a batter.
   d. incorporating a great deal of air into a batter.
3. When working with gelatin, it is necessary to
   a. first soften the gelatin in a cool liquid.
   b. break the sheets into small pieces.
   c. combine gelatin granules with sugar.
   d. add a hot liquid to the gelatin.
4. A strengthener is used in a dough to make the finished product
   a. easy to slice.
   b. stable so that it will not collapse when removed from the oven.
   c. golden brown and tender.
   d. all of the above.
5. Sugar added to a batter may make the batter
   a. soft and sticky before baking.
   b. brittle and difficult to hold for long periods after baking.
   c. pale in color.
   d. golden brown and moist, as well as attracting moisture to keep the product fresher longer.
6. Ingredients used to flavor a batter will usually
   a. have little influence on the type of leavener used in the batter or dough.
   b. make the finished product more expensive.
   c. have to be ground fine so that they will not cause the item to collapse during baking.
   d. have little effect on the batter itself during the mixing, shaping, and baking process, but will have a big effect on the way the finished item tastes.

True/False

1. _____ A shortening ingredient is always made from vegetable oil.
2. _____ It is important to prepare the pan properly, according to the type of batter being baked.
3. _____ Eggs can act as both strengtheners and shorteners.
4. _____ Fondant should be heated to around 104°F so that it can be used as a glaze or coating.
5. _____ Items that will rise during baking, especially those made from puff pastry, should always be baked in a convection oven.
6. _____ Creaming is the process of blending a granular sugar with a fat until it is smooth, light, and creamy.
7. _____ Leavening is the process of introducing air into a batter through the use of chemical, organic, or physical leaveners.
8. _____ The thickness of the baking pan or sheet has very little effect on the ultimate outcome of a baked item.

9. _____ The only reason to add sugar, syrups, honey, or other sweeteners to a batter is to make them taste sweet after they are baked.

10. _____ In order for yeast to grow properly and allow the dough to rise, it requires food, moisture, and the right temperature range.

Fill in the Blank

1. When a shaped dough is slashed so that air can escape during baking, this is known as _____.
2. When gelatin has been properly softened in cold water and then heated gently to dissolve the granules, it has been _____.
3. _____ is the process where sugar is heated enough to become brown and develop a rich flavor.
4. One of the most important ingredients in many baked goods is flour because the proteins in the flour develop a structure that is sometimes referred to as _____.
5. If a cake has been prepared in advance and frozen, it should be carefully checked for freshness and then brushed with _____ to add some moisture.
6. It is best to sift dry ingredients such as flour or cocoa powder _____.

Discussion

1. Describe the procedure for tempering chocolate.
2. What are three different ways to use tempered chocolate?
3. Describe the correct way to prepare pans to bake different types of baked goods.
4. Why is scaling so important? What might happen if items are not properly scaled?
5. How is arrowroot added to a hot liquid? What is the reason for using this thickener?
6. Describe how a shortening ingredient works in a batter. Describe the difference between a batter or dough that has had the shortener completely worked in and one that has not.

What Went Wrong?

1. A bavarian cream made with gelatin did not properly set, and there is a tough, rubbery, grainy layer at the bottom of the mold.
2. A cake formula was adapted to meet the needs of a special diet. The end result was a tough, rubbery cake that had no noticeable crumb.
3. A pancake batter was prepared in the morning and then left on a shelf over the griddle. By the end of the breakfast service period, the pancakes were flat and not as fluffy as those made earlier in the day.

Chapter 30

Yeast Doughs

This chapter covers the procedures used to bake yeast doughs of various sorts. The ability to bake breads is not a mysterious talent; anyone can learn to handle yeast, sponges, and sourdough starters properly, as long as certain rules are observed—controlling temperatures correctly, preventing the yeast from either dying or growing out of control, properly shaping and proofing the dough, and baking it correctly.

After reading and studying this chapter, you should be able to:

1. Name the two types of yeast doughs: lean and rich.
2. Describe the characteristics of both lean and rich doughs, and name examples of each.
3. Explain the importance of properly scaling ingredients for yeast doughs.
4. Name two types of yeast used in the professional bakeship, and describe the correct procedures for working with yeast and proofing it.
5. Identify some of the differences between a sponge and a sourdough starter, and explain when and why each one might be used.
6. Describe and follow the straight dough mixing method for yeast doughs.
7. Name some of the shapes used for yeast doughs, and describe the way to properly shape doughs for baking.
8. Explain what is meant by benchproofing and oven spring.
9. Describe a properly baked bread of good quality.

Matching

1. _____ Sponge

   a. Dough that has not risen sufficiently.

2. _____ Underfermented

   b. Second rising of dough, after it has been shaped and placed in pans, done either in a proofbox or on the work bench.

3. _____ Baguette

   c. An additional step in the straight dough mixing method, used with low gluten flours, such as oat or rye.

4. _____ Steam-generating

   d. The additional rise of the dough once it is placed in a hot oven to bake.

5. _____ Benchproofing

   e. A technique used to create an escape hatch for steam as the bread bakes.

6. _____ Oven spring

   f. A cabinet where dough is allowed to rise in carefully controlled temperature and humidity.

7. _____ Brioche

8. _____ Docking

9. _____ Punching down

10. _____ Proofbox

g. One of the possible shapes for a lean dough; typically called French bread, it is a long, skinny loaf.

h. A rich dough that should be baked in pans that are greased and lined with parchment.

i. A type of oven used for doughs that should have very crisp crusts.

j. Pressing the dough after the first rising, to allow the gas to escape, before shaping and benchproofing.

Multiple Choice

1. A dough that has been allowed to rise too long will
   a. have a yeasty flavor, with a taste similar to beer.
   b. be very large and puffy after it is baked.
   c. have a tough crust.
   d. have a gray streak on the inside.
2. When dough has been sufficiently kneaded, it should be
   a. stiff and easy to tear into pieces.
   b. soft and wet to the touch.
   c. smooth, elastic, and satiny to the touch.
   d. ready to bake.
3. A dough that was baked in an oven that was not hot enough
   a. will have a pale color.
   b. will have an uncooked streak in the center.
   c. will taste like dough.
   d. will not bake in the interior.
4. Adding too much salt to the dough could make it
   a. rise too much.
   b. salty, and also kill enough yeast so that the dough becomes flat.
   c. dry and crumbly.
   d. sticky and difficult to work with.
5. Proofing is done to
   a. make sure that the yeast is alive.
   b. allow the dough to rise the first time.
   c. allow the dough to rise the second time, in the pans.
   d. all of the above.

True/False

1. _____ Bread made from yeast that is too old is typically referred to as "underfermented."

2. _____ Yeast should be kept refrigerated until immediately before it is added to the dough.

3. _____ A sourdough starter's flavor depends on the type of wild yeast spores naturally present in the air.

4. _____ Docking is a technique that is used primarily as a decoration.

5. _____ Lean doughs usually do not contain a great deal of butters, oils, sugar, egg yolks, or cream.

6. _____ A yeast dough is punched down after the dough slowly returns to its original shaped after being pressed with a finger.

7. _____ A sponge is another name for a sourdough starter.

8. _____ Benchproofing occurs after the dough has risen once, been shaped, and placed in pans.

9. _____ A proof box is where yeast doughs undergo the second rise.

10. _____ The straight mix method may be used for lean doughs only.

Fill in the Blank

1. A traditional sourdough starter relies upon the presence of the _____ for its special flavor.
2. Doughs made with low gluten flours, such as _____, will often require a percentage of _____ for the best texture in the finished bread.
3. Yeast can be killed by _____.
4. Yeast is _____ by cold temperatures, but it will usually not be _____.
5. Salt is important in a bread dough formula because it _____ so that the finished bread has a good texture and flavor.

Discussion

1. Describe what properly baked, good quality bread should be like.
2. Why should a restaurant consider baking its own breads, even if there is no separate bakeshop available?
3. What is the purpose of docking breads?
4. Why is it important to properly shape breads and rolls?
5. What is the purpose of punching down doughs after the initial rise?

What Went Wrong?

1. The bread is flat, with a coarse grain, and a thick crust.
2. The bread tastes fine, but it becomes stale very quickly after baking.
3. The finished bread did not have the proper volume and is crumbly after baking. It went stale very quickly, too.

Chapter 31

Quickbreads, Cakes, and Other Batters

Many of the items discussed in this chapter can easily be prepared in almost any kitchen. When a restaurant can offer freshly baked breads, muffins, and simple desserts, there is usually a greater chance to impress the customer with the quality and variety offered. The methods used to prepare cakes, including creaming, two-stage, and foaming, allow the chef a great opportunity for creativity. Pound cakes, sponge cakes, angel food cakes, jelly rolls, and layer cakes are all within the range of possibilities. Chapter 33 describes a number of different fillings and frostings that can be used to make these simple desserts seem fancier.

After reading and studying this chapter, you should be able to:

1. Name the four mixing methods described in this chapter.
2. Describe the steps for assembling mise en place and preparing batters by the straight mix method.
3. Describe the steps for assembling mise en place and preparing batters by the creaming method.
4. Describe the steps for assembling mise en place and preparing batters by the two-stage method.
5. Describe the steps for assembling mise en place and preparing batters by the foaming method.
6. Name several examples of products prepared by each of the four mixing methods.
7. Describe the steps for assembling mise en place and preparing batters and doughs for biscuits, soufflés, and steamed dessert puddings.
8. Name some of the possible benefits for a restaurant that sells "home-baked" desserts, muffins, and quickbreads.

Matching

1. _____ Crumb

    a. A term used to describe the texture of baked items.

2. _____ Quickbread

    b. A mixing method in which eggs (whole, yolks, or whites) are beaten to a foam before incorporating flour or other ingredients.

3. _____ Popovers

    c. A dessert made from a base that has been lightened with beaten egg whites and then baked until puffed.

4. _____ Foaming

    d. A type of bread made with a chemical leavener instead of yeast.

5. _____ Folding

    e. An example of a cake made by the creaming method.

6. _____ High ratio

    f. A type of cake made by the foaming method.

7. _____ Soufflé

    g. Made from a thin batter with a high percentage of eggs.

8. _____ Soda bread

    h. The action used to gently blend mixtures without losing a great deal of air from foams.

9. _____ Chiffon

    i. A cake made by the two-stage method.

10. _____ Pound cake

    j. A type of quickbread, similar to scones and biscuits.

Multiple Choice

1. If a cake made by the creaming or two-stage methods appears to have fallen during baking, it has probably
   a. been made with insufficient leaveners.
   b. been baked at a temperature that is too low.
   c. been made without enough flour.
   d. been made with too much sugar.
2. When preparing a cake by the two-stage method, you begin with all of the sifted dry ingredients in the mixing bowl and then add
   a. all of the liquid and half of the shortening.
   b. all of the eggs and a third of the shortening.
   c. half of the shortening, all of the eggs, and half of the liquid.
   d. half of the blended liquid ingredients and all of the shortening.
3. When making a cake by the warm foaming method, the eggs and sugar should be
   a. heated over a hot-water bath to about 100°F.
   b. beaten to make a thick foam that forms ribbons when dropped from the beater.
   c. properly measured and used in the correct ratio.
   d. all of the above.
4. When preparing biscuits, it is important to
   a. have the butter or shortening cold.
   b. blend the dough until it is very smooth.
   c. knead the dough until it is elastic.
   d. bake the biscuits on ungreased, unlined sheet pans.
5. A steamed pudding has
   a. a relatively low percentage of eggs and sugar.
   b. a good chance of deflating after it is removed from the oven because the base is usually a simple purée of fruit.
   c. a physical leavener (beaten egg whites), which gives the pudding its light texture.
   d. been replaced by soufflés on all contemporary menus.

True/False

1. _____ High ratio cakes are made by the same mixing method as a pound cake.

2. _____ The foaming mixing method is used to prepare soufflés.

3. _____ Dessert soufflés rely on egg whites to provide their structure, as well as the leavening agent.

4. _____ The two-stage method contains a very high percentage of sugar in order to bolster its keeping ability.

5. _____ When the butter and sugar are properly creamed together, the next step for a pound cake is to incorporate the sifted dry ingredients.

6. _____ The dough for biscuits, scones, and soda breads should be kneaded repeatedly until the dough is springy and elastic.

7. _____ In the straight mix method, all liquid ingredients are combined and then added all at once to the combined dry ingredients.

8. _____ The reason for creaming together butter and sugar in a pound cake is to create a fine crumb and a dense, rich texture.

9. _____ Most batters used to make quickbreads, muffins, and cakes require a chemical leavener, such as baking powder or baking soda.

10. _____ Steamed puddings should be dense and more like a custard than a soufflé.

Fill in the Blank

1. An improperly mixed cupcake might have _____.
2. A type of leavener most often used in quickbreads and cake batters is _____.
3. The mixing method that calls for all of the ingredients to be mixed together at once is the _____.
4. Examples of cakes made by the foaming method include _____.
5. When creaming the butter and sugar together in a cake batter, you should select the _____ for the mixing machine.

Discussion

1. A cake is baked at a temperature that is too high. What are the likely characteristics of the cake after baking?
2. What ingredients might cause the crust of a batter cake, muffin, or quickbread to be darker than the interior (note that this is not necessarily a fault)?
3. Why is the two-stage method for making cakes desirable? What is different about this method?
4. Describe the method for preparing biscuits.
5. Describe what a cake made by the creaming mixing method should be like after proper mixing and baking.
6. Briefly explain the method for a straight mix method batter.

What Went Wrong?

1. A blueberry cake tastes fine, but all of the berries are on the bottom of the cake.
2. A layer cake has a very coarse and uneven grain.

Chapter 32

Pastry Doughs and Cookies

This chapter introduces the techniques used to make pie dough, croissants, Danish, and puff pastry dough. These pastry doughs are used to make such items as tarts, pies, and French pastries. Once the basic technique for making these doughs is mastered, it is possible to make not only many different types of doughs, but also different desserts.

After reading and studying this chapter, you should be able to:

1. Prepare both flaky and mealy pie dough.
2. Explain the procedure for rolling out pie dough and for making bottom and top layers and lattice crusts.
3. Fill and top a variety of pies and tarts.
4. Prepare three types of roll-in doughs: croissant, danish, and puff pastry.
5. Properly shape and fill roll-in doughs, to create a variety of items.
6. Describe the method for working with phyllo dough.
7. Describe the procedure for blitz puff pastry, and explain when its use is appropriate.
8. Describe the steps in making, shaping, and baking pâte à choux.
9. Name some of the types of cookies and how they are prepared.
10. Name and describe a variety of fillings and toppings for pastries.

Matching

1. _____ Baking blind
2. _____ Eclair
3. _____ Roll-in
4. _____ Lattice
5. _____ French pastries
6. _____ Book-fold
7. _____ Blitz puff pastry
8. _____ Tart pans
9. _____ Pithiviers
10. _____ Frangipane

a. Another name for a four-fold used when preparing puff pastry.

b. A top crust made by cutting strips of dough and weaving them.

c. Straight-sided pans with removable bottoms.

d. A classic French pastry made with puff pastry and almond paste.

e. A type of shell made from pâte à choux.

f. Made in the same way as a flaky pie dough, but with a higher percentage of fat.

g. A filling for petit fours made from almond paste.

h. The name given to the butter and flour mixture incorporated into a dough by folding and rolling it into layers.

i. Pastries made from puff pastry, filled and glazed.

j. Procedure for pre-baking a pie shell.

Multiple Choice

1. A Danish dough is similar to a croissant dough because both of them require
   a. yeast in the basic dough.
   b. a roll-in made by working butter or shortening until it is smooth, elastic, and pliable, but still cool.
   c. careful control of temperatures while preparing, shaping, and proofing the doughs.
   d. all of the above.
2. The visual clue that pâte à choux is properly baked and ready to remove from the oven is
   a. the items have nearly doubled in volume.
   b. the items have a light golden color.
   c. there are no beads of moisture on the edges of the items.
   d. a small hole develops in the bottom of each item to release steam.
3. There are many different ways to prepare cookies. Some of them are
   a. drop cookies, packaged cookies, and freezer cookies.
   b. bagged cookies, boxed cookies, and bar cookies.
   c. spritz cookies, filled cookies, and icebox cookies.
   d. butter cookies, almond cookies, and sheet cookies.
4. Blitz puff pastry is
   a. essentially the same as flaky pie dough in preparation and handling.
   b. used where the item requires an absolutely even rise and regular appearance.
   c. made with shortening instead of butter.
   d. made with eggs.
5. The way to be certain that you will get the proper results when working with pastry dough is to
   a. have all ingredients at room temperature before beginning to work.
   b. control temperatures carefully during mixing, shaping, and baking.
   c. properly sift dry ingredients at least twice.
   d. use marble slabs to roll out doughs.

True/False

1. _____ Tarts almost always have a double crust.

2. _____ Although frozen phyllo dough usually has a good quality, most kitchens will make their own because it is quick and almost fool-proof.

3. _____ If the fat has been worked more completely into the dough, the end result will be crumbly and mealy, rather than flaky.

4. _____ Baking blind means to bake the dough with a filling until browned.

5. _____ The roll-in used for puff pastry should be chilled until it is firm before continuing with the procedure for preparing the dough.

6. _____ Adding sugar to a basic pie dough could make it darker in color, with a crumbly texture.

7. _____ It is a good idea to completely dissolve the salt in cold liquid when making pie dough.

8. _____ When properly baked, the pie dough should appear dry.

9. _____ French pastries usually are made with marzipan and chantilly.

10. _____ Pâte à choux is the same thing as puff pastry.

Fill in the Blank

1. Three different terms used for a dough that is typically stretched until extremely thin and brushed with butter or oil between layers are _____.
2. An example of a baked item made from 1-2-3 dough is _____.
3. A pie dough that is made by working together the flour and shortening until the mixture takes on a golden or yellow color is _____.
4. Another way to refer to a basic pie dough is _____. This refers to the ratio of _____, _____, and _____.
5. Each time the dough is rolled out and then folded when preparing puff pastry, croissant dough, or danish, it is known as a _____.

Discussion

1. Describe some of the ways that cookies can be made, and when they might be served.
2. Why is it important to manipulate fat the correct way when preparing pastry doughs and cookies?
3. Describe the procedure for working with phyllo dough.
4. Describe the procedure for preparing a croissant dough.
5. Describe the differences between a flaky and a mealy pie dough.
6. What is the difference between a tart and a typical "American" pie?

What Went Wrong?

1. The pie dough is very tough, both before and after it is baked.
2. The apple pie featured on the menu is always prepared by one of the line cooks. She went on vacation and, while she was away, the pantry cook baked the pies. The crust was soaked on the bottom.

Chapter 33

Dessert Sauces, Creams, and Frozen and Fruit Desserts

The ability to take plain baked goods and turn them into "pastries" requires that the chef be able to prepare a number of different items, including dessert sauces, bavarian creams, mousses, ice creams, and other frozen desserts. The skill with which they are made and used will make the difference between an ordinary dessert and a special one.

After reading and studying this chapter, you should be able to:

1. Name a number of different dessert sauces.
2. Describe the correct method for making a vanilla sauce.
3. Name the different types of buttercreams and briefly describe how they are prepared.
4. Name a number of different frozen desserts.
5. Explain what is meant by a still-frozen item.
6. Describe how to properly poach fruits.
7. Explain the procedure for assembling and decorating a torte.

Matching

1. _____ Custard sauce

2. _____ Frozen soufflé

3. _____ Italian buttercream

4. _____ Bavarian

5. _____ Torte

6. _____ Granite

7. _____ Ganache

8. _____ Sabayon

9. _____ Caramel sauce

10. _____ Pastry cream

a. A still-frozen dessert made from a flavored syrup that is scraped to form crystals before it is served.

b. A custard sauce that has been stabilized with gelatin and lightened with whipped cream.

c. A frozen dessert made by still-freezing a bavarian cream or a mousse in a mold.

d. A fragile sauce made by whipping a mixture of yolks, marsala, and sugar over a hot waterbath until thickened and foamy.

e. Buttercream made by preparing an Italian meringue and then incorporating softened butter.

f. A fancy layer cake, usually decorated.

g. A sauce made from cream and/or milk, sugar, vanilla, and eggs (and perhaps additional egg yolks).

h. A mixture of chocolate, cream, and butter, used as a glaze or to make truffles.

i. A sort of custard sauce made with flour.

j. A sauce made by cooking a sugar syrup until brown and then adding cream and/or butter.

Multiple Choice

1. Pastry cream is often considered
   a. a dessert sauce
   b. a part of the basic mise en place of the bakeshop.
   c. too difficult for most bakeshops to prepare, so it is purchased already prepared.
   d. too delicate to allow it to come to a full boil at any point during its preparation.
2. A Bavarian cream is similar to a
   a. mousse, except that a mousse does not usually contain gelatin as a stabilizer.
   b. pastry cream, made with fewer egg yolks.
   c. frozen soufflé.
   d. all of the above.
3. Buttercreams may be made by several different techniques, and are known as
   a. soft, creamy, and dense.
   b. meringue-based, custard-based, or syrup-based.
   c. French, Italian, Swiss, and German.
   d. vanilla, chocolate, and lemon.
4. Frozen desserts may be either
   a. made with cream or made with egg whites.
   b. churned in a freezer or still-frozen.
   c. served directly from the freezer or allowed to return to room temperature.
   d. flavored with chocolate or coffee.
5. The way you can tell when the gelatin has begun to set enough to add the whipped cream into a Bavarian is that
   a. the mixture is stiff enough to hold its own shape.
   b. the mixture is cool to the touch.
   c. the mixture can be removed from the bowl or other mold in one piece.
   d. the mixture mounds very slightly when dropped from a spoon.

True and False

1. _____ Crème anglaise, custard sauce, and vanilla sauce are different names for the same dessert sauce.

2. _____ A berry coulis can be made successfully with frozen berries when fresh ones are not available, but be sure that they are unsweetened.

3. _____ Once cooked, custard sauce should be quickly cooled to below 40°F.

4. _____ The more egg yolks included in a vanilla sauce, the richer and thicker the finished sauce will be.

5. _____ Another name for a particular type of chocolate sauce is ganache.

6. _____ A traditional sabayon sauce is made with Madeira wine.

7. _____ A Bavarian cream is made with whipped cream, puréed fruit, and gelatin.

8. _____ Adding sugar to a berry coulis or other fruit sauce may cause the sauce to thicken as it cools.

9. _____ Caramel sauce and butterscotch sauce both begin with a sugar syrup that has been cooked until it is a deep, golden brown.

10. _____ Pastry cream is served by itself as a dessert.

Fill in the Blank

1. A basic vanilla sauce can be altered in order to prepare a number of different items, including _____.

2. A french butter cream is made by combining _____.
3. A dessert item made by combining a custard sauce with a flavoring and then adding a foam of beaten egg whites or whipped cream is called a _____.
4. Usually, tortes are made with layers of sponge cake, also known as genoise, but it is also possible to use layers of _____.
5. Buttercreams may be used as either a _____ or a _____.

Discussion

1. When items such as stock or water are frozen, they become solid blocks that cannot be scooped up. Why doesn't this happen to ice cream or frozen soufflés?
2. What are the differences between the four types of buttercream?
3. What is the procedure for preparing a fancy torte?
4. Name several types of dessert sauces besides custard sauce.

What Went Wrong?

1. The pastry chef has prepared a poached pear dessert by gently poaching the fruit in a sugar syrup. The pear is almost crunchy after poaching.
2. The custard sauce is very thick and has an "eggy" flavor.

Introduction to the Foodservice Industry

	Matching	Multiple Choice	True/False
1.	d	a	F
2.	g	d	T
3.	a	a	F
4.	e	c	T
5.	b	d	T
6.	f	b	F
7.	c	c	F

Fill in the Blank

1. agriculture
2. indigenous
3. etiquette
4. feudalism
5. cuisine bourgeoise
6. haute cuisine
7. pasteurization
8. irradiation
9. hydroponics
10. Cuisinier

Discussion

1. Charles Ranhofer, Delmonico's Restaurant.
2. Fills in for the chef when not present. Second in command.
3. Clean, fillet, cut (etc.) all fish items; prepare sauces for fish entrées and appetizers. Saucier might assume duties.
4. Dining room manager (maître d'); wine steward (sommelier); head waiter (chef de salle); captain (chef d'etage); front waiter (chef de rang); busboy (commis de rang).
5. Cold food preparation (salads, cold appetizers, pâtés). Also, breakfast cookery. Known as "garde-manger."
6. Writer, teacher, food stylist, critic, consultants, design specialist, salespeople, research, and development.
7. Some of the separate line cook positions are combined into the duties of a single person (see diagram, p. 9).

8. More two-income families, who dine out more often; increasing percentage of customers who are concerned with nutrition; older clientele. All of these groups rely on restaurants to meet special needs, such as early bird specials, low prices, and fast service.

9. Was married to Henry IV. She is credited with introducing forks and napkins to the court. Also brought chefs with her who introduced special foods and cooking styles to the French.

10. Wrote *Le Guide Culinaire*, helped make dining in restaurants a socially acceptable thing to do; initiated the brigade system; helped simplify the preparation of foods and the menu by following some of the principles of Careme.

What Went Wrong?

Perhaps the brigade system is not being used. When an order comes in, therefore, the person who is free prepares all the food. With the brigade system in place, one person is responsible for only the grilled foods, one person for only the sautéed foods, etc. Perhaps the line cooks are not familiar with the dishes, and perhaps they are not properly trained for their position.

The Professional Chef

	Matching	Multiple Choice	True/False
1.	a	e	T
2.	e	b	F
3.	b	b	F
4.	d	b	T
5.	f		F
6.	c		T
7.	i		F
8.	h		
9.	j		
10.	g		

Fill in the Blank

1. join organizations, network, read trade journal and book, and compete
2. come first
3. Profit
4. hiding in a monastery
5. Better Business Bureau or other business people
6. Follow-the-leader

Discussion

1. Rudeness, waste of food, abuse of equipment, sexual harassment, profanity, ethnic slurs, verbal abuse.
2. Going to other restaurants; travel; joining professional organizations; joining in competitions and foodshows; taking additional courses in special subjects; subscription to trade publications.
3. Enables chef to determine what works well together, so that menus, recipes, and entire events can be planned that are appropriate and pleasing. Judgment also comes only with experience, and the goal is to grow, rather than to achieve final mastery.
4. Hat, or toque; pleats said to represent the 100 ways a chef can prepare eggs.
   Pants with houndstooth check; snaps are practical because they do not appear soiled quickly.
   Double breasted jacket; gender neutral, but able to rebutton so that chef can come into the dining room looking clean.
5. Used for record keeping, financial planning. Also can standardize recipes, introduce nutritional analysis, and do some forecasting for upcoming events. Depending upon software and links, may help with research or to find special ingredients, recipes, formulas, or contacts through data search and electronic bulletin boards.

What Went Wrong?

Lighting could have been harsh, making everyone look slightly "washed out" or "green." Chairs might not have been comfortable, so no one wanted to stay. Music could have been playing too loudly, and/or it might have been too fast, making everyone eat quickly. Menus may have been hard to read.

All of these conditions might have induced everyone to order less food (lower check average than the operator may have hoped for) because their experience was unpleasant.

Sanitation and Safety

	Matching	Multiple Choice	True/False
1.	f	d	T
2.	d	a	T
3.	i	c	F
4.	j	e	F
5.	g	b	F
6.	h		T
7.	c		T
8.	a		F
9.	b		T
10.	e		T

Fill in the Blank

1. nausea, vomiting, diarrhea, fever
2. bandaids, fingernails, earrings, hair
3. Heimlich maneuver
4. Intoxication
5. two or more people, health officials
6. fission

Discussion

1. In dry storage, keep room ventilated, practice FIFO, keep foods off the flour, keep vents and fans unblocked.
   In refrigerated storage, separate raw and cooked foods, use drip pans to prevent cross contamination, use separate storage for dairy items, meats, fish, and produce whenever possible.
   Label and date foods clearly so they can be used while still safe and of good quality.
2. Communication, so that everyone knows about hot, heavy, greasy, or dangerous situations.
   Proper instruction in the use and cleaning of equipment.
   Have first aid available.
   Someone should know first aid, and telephone numbers should be posted.
   Fire extinguishers should meet fire codes and be inspected properly.
3. Wiping eyes, mouth, scratching head, or handling money, and then handling food without washing hands in between.
   Using the cutting board for chicken to prepare a salad of raw chopped vegetables without sanitizing the board between uses.
   Allowing raw foods to drip onto cooked foods below them.

4. The spores are capable of protecting the bacteria from being totally wiped out due to adverse situations. The spores can resist extreme temperatures or dehydration and can allow the bacteria to resume life cycles when favorable conditions return.

What Went Wrong?

Improper handling of potentially hazardous foods that may have been allowed to reach and stay in the danger zone for too long.

Improper sanitation of tools and equipment during preparation; cross-contamination when personnel failed to remember proper personal hygiene.

Elderly are often more at risk from food-borne illness than other groups and could easily wind up hospitalized.

This involves enough people and would be verified by health officials as an official outbreak. That would make the restaurant liable and could lead to bad publicity, fines, or other measures.

Nutrition and Nutritional Cooking

	Matching	Multiple Choice	True/False
1.	d	c	F
2.	f	a	F
3.	j	d	T
4.	g	a	T
5.	c	c	T
6.	a	e	F
7.	b		T
8.	i		T
9.	h		F
10.	e		F
11.			T

Fill in the Blank

1. Carbohydrates, glycogen, or glucose are all acceptable answers.
2. Palm oil, palm kernel oil, coconut oil
3. calcium
4. Smoke-roasting
5. a variety of foods
6. reduction of calories (not below 1200 calories per day however), exercise

Discussion

1. Would not receive full array of nutrients needed.
2. Solid at room temperature, usually of animal origin.
3. Body is capable of making other 14.
4. Age, gender, exercise, stress, consumption of foods high in saturated fat and cholesterol, and lack of fiber in the diet.
5. Typical diet is high in calories, total fats, saturated fats, cholesterol, and sodium, is low in fiber and complex carbohydrates, and contains a great deal of refined sugars.

   Recommendations are to keep the percentage of calories from protein in our diets about the same, but to reduced our consumption of refined sugars from 24% to 10% or less, reduce fat calories from 42% to 30% or less, and increase complex carbohydrate calories from 22% to 48%.

6. There are recommended numbers of servings in each of the four groups, based on age and gender.
7. Be aware of the fat content of foods; choose low-sodium, low-fat foods where possible; purchase USDA Choice instead of Prime; use whole grains instead of milled or refined grains.
8. Additives are any of a number ingredients used to increase flavor of keeping properties. Some "natural" examples include sugar and salt. Not all additives are harmful, but some are. It is important to be aware of what a special brand contains.
9. Proper technique will bring out flavor without hiding behind salt, butter, cream, or sauces; cooking vegetables quickly in as little liquid as possible makes them more nutritious, and they will also look and taste better. Use of herbs, spices, and other special ingredients can give flavor without fat. (For more examples, see p. 45.)

What Went Wrong?

Properly presented foods can meet the suggested portion sizes without looking skimpy. By slicing and fanning the food, placing it on a bed of pasta, vegetables, or grains, and adding additional vegetables to the plate, an impression of bounty is given and the expectation that it will be filling and delicious becomes a self-fulfilling prophesy.

Equipment Identification

	Matching	Multiple Choice	True/False
1.	f	d	T
2.	b	a	F
3.	h	b	F
4.	g	d	T
5.	a	a	T
6.	j		T
7.	c		T
8.	i		F
9.	e		F
10.	d		F

Fill in the Blank

1. Scoops, ladels, scales
2. Arkansas stone
3. tourné knife
4. hollow ground knife
5. batterie de cuisine
6. melon baller (or parisienne scoop), rotary peeler, thremometers, pastry bag and tips
7. instant-reading, candy, deep fat
8. copper

Discussion

1. Used for a variety of tasks; most often used; should last a lifetime; represents an investment in professional tools.
2. Walk-ins situated to allow deliveries to be stored without interrupting work in the kitchen; smaller units or reach-ins close to prep areas; refrigerated cabinets and drawers on the line to keep foods for service at safe temperatures.
3. Hold the knife at a 20-degree angle to the steel for honing, and draw the blade in a downward motion over the surface of the steel, making sure the entire length of the blade is honed. (Photo sequence on p. 55.)
   Secure the stone on a surface so that it will not slip. Push or pull the blade over the surface of the stone so that the edge of the blade is in contact with the stone. Repeat an even number of strokes on each side until the stone is properly sharpened. (Photo sequence on p. 54.)

4. Each heats foods differently and gives a special texture to the finished item. Convection ovens work rapidly and evenly by forcing the hot air to circulate with fans. Deck ovens are good for preparing hearth breads; the heat source is located below the floor of the stove. Pizza ovens are similar; essentially, they are a number of shallow ovens that can be stacked on top of one another.

5. Transmits heat evenly and rapidly. Extremely responsive to changes in cooking temperature.
   Expensive, difficult, and time-consuming to maintain.

6. Taper-ground blade made from a single sheet of metal that should take an edge easily and keep it a reasonable length of time; full tang to assure stability; hard wood handle to make knife comfortable to hold; smooth rivets flush with surface of handle so that dirt, grease, and pathogens won't collect as easily; bolster at the heel of the blade, which is usually the sign of a well-made durable knife.

7. Graduated measuring pitchers, ounce/pound and gram/kilogram scales, portion scales, cups, measuring spoons, and thermometers.

8. Straining various ingredients and making smooth sauces, soups, beverages, desserts. Size of opening in metal or weave of mesh will determine how smooth the final product is.

What Went Wrong?

Might have forgotten to turn off and unplug machine.

Might have let his attention wander.

Might have disassembled the slicer improperly.

Might never have been properly instructed in the correct procedure for use and cleaning of large equipment.

Meats, Poultry, and Game Identification

	Matching	Multiple Choice	True/False
1.	l	a	T
2.	e	b	T
3.	k	c	T
4.	f	d	F
5.	d	b	F
6.	a		
7.	c		
8.	m		
9.	b		
10.	g		
11.	i		
12.	h		
13.	j		

Fill in the Blank

1. organ meats; muscle meats
2. domesticated
3. lamb; mutton
4. mandatory
5. moisture; weight; yield

Discussion

1. Depends upon menu items, skill level of kitchen staff, and budget.
2. Store loosely wrapped in butcher paper under refrigeration, with drip trays underneath.
3. Cryovac is a type of packaging for meats that is air-tight and made up of several layers.
4. At various points on farm; in pens at slaughterhouse, before and after slaughtering.
5. Grades are determined by trained USDA inspector who checks for confirmation, yield, and other factors.
6. Prime, Choice, Select, Standard, Commercial, Utility, Cutter, and Canner.
7. Prime, Choice, Good, Standard, and Utility.
8. Shape of carcass, relation of usable meat to bone and fat, marbling, size, and weight.
9. A, B, and C.

10. Freedom from broken bones, pinfeathers, and down; ratio of meat to bone; shape of carcass.
11. Shoulder, rib, loin, and leg.
12. One of the first cuts made to divide a carcass into sections.
13. The amount of work done (cutting, trimming, portioning, etc.) will determine cost to purchaser.
14. All types.
15. Yield grade is a specific factor that has been assigned to show the usable meat vs. trim.
16. Rib and shoulder or chuck.
17. Round and loin.
18. Left to hang in controlled environment until meat darkens, looses moisture, and changes flavor. May also be done in Cryovac. Yield is significantly reduced.
19. From 1 day up to 16 weeks.
20. Shoulder (chuck), shank, rack (rib), loin, and leg.
21. Offal (cuts such as brain, sweetbreads, liver, and tongue).
22. Ham (leg), shoulder butt, and loin.
23. Age; mutton is over one year.
24. Would change both flavor and color of meat.
25. Rib (rack), square-cut shoulder, breast, shank, loin, and leg.
26. A type of farm-raised venison.
27. Lower in both, significantly.
28. Usually farm-raised, available year round.
29. Loin is usually roasted, grilled, or sautéed quickly; legs are cooked by moist-heat methods.
30. Raised in open yards where they can walk freely and get more excercies.
31. Size, age, and maturity. Broiler, fryer, roasting, stewing.
32. Domestic poultry have been specially bred to have certain characteristics; game birds retain some of their "wild" nature, as well as a more developed flavor.
33. Innards such as brain, tongue, liver, sweetbreads, calf's tail, kidneys, and tripe. Growing consumer acceptance.
34. Organ meats (liver, kidneys, brain, sweetbreads) and muscle meats (tripe, tongue, tail, heart).
35. Specially slaughtered, bled, and fabricated to meet specific dietary regulations.
36. Too difficult to remove all the veins and arteries without mangling the meat.
37. Tender, flavorful, best quality.
38. Purchase appropriate cuts, increase yield, and reduce waste.

What Went Wrong?

1. Venison is often more exercised than domestic animals; might be better to braise in a liquid or to bard or lard before roasting.
2. Used an older bird; as bird ages, loses tenderness and requires long, slow cooking in liquid, but develops a fuller flavor.

Fish and Shellfish Identification

	Matching	Multiple Choice	True/False
1.	e	d	T
2.	d	b	F
3.	h	c	T
4.	c	a	T
5.	k	b	F
6.	i		
7.	f		
8.	l		
9.	b		
10.	a		
11.	m		
12.	g		
13.	j		

Fill in the Blank

1. belly burn; viscera
2. shucking; liquor
3. name of the beds
4. soft-shelled crabs
5. salted roe; sturgeon

Discussion

1. Live shellfish should move; shells should close when tapped together; fresh clean odor.
2. See *The New Professional Chef* (pp. 86 and 87).
3. Makes a better contact, without piercing or bruising; drains away, keeping fish dryer.
4. Daily.
5. In burlap sacks.
6. In plastic containers set into ice.
7. Wrapped in seaweed or in cardboard boxes under refrigeration if a tank is not available.
8. Under 0°F.
9. Fish that has been thawed and refrozen, improperly handled, stored, shipped, or processed.

10. See *The New Professional Chef* (pp. 87 and 88).
11. See *The New Professional Chef* (p. 88).
12. The market form (round fish) is a whole fish with viscera intact. The round fish as a category of fish is as described in question 11.
13. Whelk is smaller and grayish in color when compared to the true conch from the Caribbean.
14. Shark, rays or skates, and monkfish have cartilege instead of bones.
15. See *The New Professional Chef* (p. 94 and 95).
16. By the name of the bed they were harvested from
17. bay, sea, and calico. See description on p. 96 in *The New Professional Chef.*
18. scallops
19. See *The New Professional Chef* (p. 96).
20. Crayfish are usually fresh water, and lobster is usually salt water.
21. Female has soft appendages on stomach, tail is broader, and has roe.
22. Average number of shrimp in a pound.

What Went Wrong

1. Did not properly apply the seven steps for checking fish quality (see p. 86).
2. Not able to match quality of fish (in terms of texture, leanness, or oiliness) with a cooking method.

Fruit, Vegetable, and
Fresh Herb Identification

	Matching	Multiple Choice	True/False
1.	h	d	T
2.	g	c	F
3.	d	a	F
4.	a	d	T
5.	c	b	T
6.	i		
7.	e		
8.	f		
9.	b		

Fill in the Blank

1. summer fruits; winter fruits
2. thin-skinned, thick-skinned, bitter
3. drier, more acidic; dessert
4. cantaloupes, watermelons, winter melons, musk melons
5. natural sugars; starch

Discussion

1. When it is in season.
2. Fresher; may be less expensive because shipping fees are less; may be able to get special produce not available elsewhere; support local economy.
3. Growing vegetables and herbs in nutrient-rich water instead of soil. Easy to clean. Have very delicate flavors.
4. 40°to 45°F and humidity of 80 to 90%. Bananas, onions, apples, and potatoes are exceptions.
5. To prevent spoilage, growth of molds, etc.
6. Room temperature.
7. Lemon and melons give off; apples and cherries absorb.
8. Summer fruits, which do not keep well; winter fruits which can be stored over the winter if properly handled.
9. Check bottom of container to see if berries are moldy, squashed, or overripe.
10. Thin-skinned, thick-skinned, and bitter.
11. Cantaloupes, musk melon, watermelon, and winter melon.
12. Freestone, where flesh pulls cleanly away, and clingstone, where flesh adheres tightly to the stone.

13. Stem or stalk.
14. Almost always picked green and allowed to ripen in transit.
15. Brassica (but often thought of as roots or tubers).
16. Winter squash have thick skin and large seeds and are picked mature; summer squash have thin, edible skins and smaller seeds and are picked immature.
17. Wild and domestic, fresh and dried, canned and frozen.
18. Allowed to ripen on the plant.
19. In the seeds.
20. Sweetest and most tender then.
21. Pods are inedible or indigestible.
22. Root vegetables are a part of the root system, acting as storage; tubers are an enlarged root actually capable of generating a new plant.
23. Dry and unpeeled; if greens are attached, they should be trimmed away.
24. Leaves of aromatic plants.
25. Smell, color, feel, and no wilting or brown spots.
26. Select according to special flavor affinities; mince or cut into chiffonade as close to time they are added to a dish as possible, add at the end of cooking time for hot dishes. Cold dishes should be allowed time for the flavor of the herb to develop.
27. Loosely wrapped in damp paper or cloth, or with stems in fresh water.
28. Quality of locally grown items may be better; may be able to arrange suitable deliveries so that items are not overpurchased.

What Went Wrong?

1. May have stored fruit improperly, in a place that was too warm; also likely that the ethylene gas from the bananas hastened spoiling.
2. Tomatoes picked green ripe are usually not as flavorful as fresh, local tomatoes that are in season, or even canned tomatoes that were processed when they were fully ripe. Should consider alternatives to fresh but tasteless product.

Dairy, Cheese, and Egg Identification

	Matching	Multiple Choice	True/False
1.	g	b	F
2.	j	c	F
3.	a	d	F
4.	c	a	T
5.	i	c	F
6.	b	a	T
7.	h	d	T
8.	d		F
9.	e		F
10.	f		T

Fill in the Blank

1. from the outside in
2. a culture to lowfat or skim milk.
3. curds
4. ultrapasteurization
5. sorbet
6. Vitamin A, Vitamin D

Discussion

1. Removing the fat also removes these fat soluble vitamins.
2. The ice cream "weeps" as it melts; it melts slowly in the mouth and has a gritty texture; there is too much air in the ice cream.
3. They are important ingredients in other preparations. They can be used to make foams, sauces, soufflés, desserts, meringues, and mayonnaise.
4. It has usually been stabilized, and may not whip as easily or to as great a volume as heavy cream, which is not stabilized.
5. Salt might tend to mask the off odors that indicate butter has begun to lose its quality. Eventually, the butter will become rancid with a sour aroma like that of curdled milk. Also may make finished dish too salty.

What Went Wrong?

Milk and other dairy items deteriorate rapidly when they are stored improperly. To maintain best quality, store at 35° F.

Nonperishable Goods Identification

	Matching	Multiple Choice	True/False
1.	d	a	T
2.	i	c	F
3.	e	d	F
4.	b	b	T
5.	h	d	F
6.	a	c	T
7.	f		T
8.	j		F
9.	c		
10.	g		

Fill in the Blank

1. Japanese
2. carob
3. maple syrup
4. juniper berries
5. Tellicherry
6. 3½
7. deodorization

Discussion

1. Stores well; cooks quickly; comes in range of shapes, sizes, and flavors; base for a number of different preparations from a variety of cuisines.
2. See Table 10-1 on pages 145–46.
3. The seeds from pod-producing plants.
4. It is crushed into successively smaller particles.
5. See Table 10-4, page 152.
6. See Table 10-8, page 157.
7. A powder made from dried sweet peppers; may be mild, sweet, or hot. Hungarian paprika is considered superior in flavor.

What Went Wrong?

Beans may have been moldy, dirty, and old. The older the bean, the longer it will take to cook.

Meat Fabrication

	Matching	Multiple Choice	True/False
1.	g	c	T
2.	b	a	F
3.	e	b	T
4.	a	d	T
5.	h		F
6.	i		F
7.	d		T
8.	f		
9.	j		
10.	c		

Fill in the Blank

1. pounding
2. filet mignon, chateubriand, noisette, medallion, and tournedos
3. paillard
4. help it cook more evenly and look more attractive
5. disjointing

Discussion

1. Terms are different, and it is important to be able to communicate exact needs in terms that will allow purveyor to provide the desired cuts.
2. Able to save and use trim for other purposes; have more control over size and shape of meats; may be able to save money.
3. The soft substance found in the center of bones; is removed by soaking in salt water and pushing marrow out of bone.
4. Might smell of urine. Problem is eliminated by cutting away all fat and veins and possibly by blanching.
5. Meat cut into strips, about ⅛-inch thick, ½-inch wide, and 1 to 2 inches long.)
6. Cutting board, sharp knife, steel, butcher's twine, and meat pounder.

What Went Wrong?

Chef didn't specify exact needs; no one knew how to cut meat so someone ought to take a class and learn basic skills; waste of material and loss of profit.

Poultry Fabrication

	Matching	Multiple Choice	True/False
1.	b	b	F
2.	c	c	F
3.	e	d	T
4.	a	b	T
5.	d	a	T
6.			F
7.			T
8.			T

Multiple Choice

1. b
2. c
3. d
4. b
5. a

Fill in the Blank

1. heel
2. natural seams
3. make a pocket in the skin of the thigh to hold the drumstick in place
4. to remove the first two wing joints
5. suprême
6. trussed

Discussion

1. Chickens are similar to most other forms of poultry; once you are familiar with the terms, bones, and configuration of chicken, the same techniques can easily be applied to other birds.
2. Less waste, greater profit; bones used for stock, and wings for hors d'oeuvre and snack foods; trim used for forcemeats; if cost to customer of an entrée featuring only the breast can cover the food cost for the entire bird, any use made of the other parts of the bird can be clear profit.
3. Ducks needed for an evening's service are roasted in advance; bird is halved and partially or full deboned, depending upon the style used by the restaurant, and then reheated in a hot oven.

4. Two wings, two drumsticks, two thighs, two pieces of breast; used often with broilers and fryers; useful for birds to be grilled, sautéed, panfried, deep-fried, stewed, or braised.

What Went Wrong?

Train someone to cut up birds to fabricate the pieces needed; save trim and bones to made stock for soups.

Fish and Shellfish Fabrication

	Matching	Multiple Choice	True/False
1.	j	b	T
2.	g	b	F
3.	b	a	F
4.	h	d	T
5.	a	c	F
6.	i	b	T
7.	e	d	F
8.	d		T
9.	f		
10.	c		

Fill in the Blank

1. pinbones
2. picking crayfish
3. mantle
4. ink sac
5. roe
6. tentacles

Discussion

1. Supplies of some fish, usually the most familiar, are dwindling, and unusual species are becoming both more available and more acceptable to the customer. Knowing how to work with a wide variety of fish opens up the options available to the chef. Also, if the fish is cut into the desired portion, any trim, including the bones, can be used to help cut down on food cost and increase profit.
2. Fillet, tranche, goujon, goujonette, and paupiette.
3. Tuna, swordfish, mahi-mahi, salmon, halibut, and shark.
4. See pages 188 through 191.

What Went Wrong

The chef was not able to take advantage of the readily available fish because the menu "locked him in" to serving only lemon sole. Instead of being able to offer a special, he was simply unable to offer a fish entrée. Perhaps the chef turned down the roughy out of fear that it would be difficult to fabricate or that the customers wouldn't like it. At any rate, sales were probably affected, and quite possible customers were not pleased.

Mise en Place

	Matching	Multiple Choice	True/False
1.	e	b	F
2.	d	e	T
3.	h	e	T
4.	a	e	T
5.	k	b	T
6.	c	c	
7.	i		
8.	f		
9.	l		
10.	b		
11.	j		
12.	m		
13.	n		
14.	g		

Fill in the Blank

1. Sugar; acidic
2. different
3. milk solids
4. Reduction
5. just before service

Discussion

1. Refer to chart on page 207.
2. Swivel bladed peeler, in a gas flame, broiler, deepfry; char surface, then sweat in container and peel away skin.
3. Piqué is studded with clove and bay leaf; brulée is halved and charred.
4. Peel tomato by plunging in boiling water and then shocking; cut in half (across belly for beefsteak or slicing tomatoes, from blossom to stem end for plum), remove core, squeeze out seeds, and chop flesh.
5. Bain-marie is either a stainless steel insert or a hot water bath used to gently cook items such as custards in the oven.

6. Rondelle and oblique.

7. Melt and allow foam to come to top and solids to separate to bottom, skim off foam, and ladle off clarified butter, leaving solids behind. Or melt completely until butter separates as above, pour into bain-marie, chill until solid, poke, and drain off solids and water.

8. Be sure that bowl and whip are completely clean (may be a good idea to rinse with white vinegar), have egg whites at room temperature, begin whipping at moderate speed, and increase speed as foam thickens until desired "peak" is reached.

9. Traps some but not all of steam, allows foods to cook gently without forming a tough skin on top.

10. Soften gelatin in cold water, dissolve gently over warm water bath, and then add to liquid.

What Went Wrong?

(Chopped garlic, shallots, minced herbs, tomato concassé, clarified butter, roux, beurre manié, roasted peppers, cut and prepped vegetables, appropriate garnish for main items, sauce components, including chilled butter for sauces to be finished with butter, etc.)

Stocks

	Matching	Multiple Choice	True/False
1.	g	b	T
2.	c	d	T
3.	f	d	F
4.	a	a	F
5.	h	d	F
6.	e		
7.	b		
8.	d		

Fill in the Blanks

1. proteins
2. coagulated albumin
3. strong color
4. Remouillage
5. blanched, browned, sweated

Discussion

1. Base for soup, sauces, braises, and stews.
2. Major flavoring ingredients (bones, trim, or vegetables), liquid (water, remouillage, or stock), and mirepoix.
3. Roasted to give rich brown color and increased flavor by roasting in hot oven until good color is achieved; blanched by placing in cold water, bringing to a boil, and then draining and rinsing to remove impurities; sweating in covered pot to speed extraction.
4. Refer to complete method, pages 236–37, and short version on p. 239.
5. Flavor, color, aroma, and clarity.
6. See variations on page 243.
7. Because they are used for a variety of applications.
8. Estouffade is a type of stock, typically used to prepare sauce Espagnol.

What Went Wrong?

Stock may have been allowed to boil during preparation. It was probably not properly cooled, so souring began when it was placed in cooler, a strong likelihood if the stock was strained immediately into plastic storage containers. Also, if the stock had not been properly labeled and dated, it is possible that this stock was not that made yesterday, and could be much older.

Soups

Matching	Multiple Choice	True/False
1. j	b	F
2. e	d	T
3. h	e	F
4. b	d	T
5. c	c	F
6. i		
7. k		
8. f		
9. d		
10. a		
11. g		

Fill in the Blanks

1. thicker
2. boiling
3. heavy cream
4. "as is"
5. Quality stocks

Discussion

1. Major flavoring ingredient, aromatics, and liquid.
2. See points listed on page 250.
3. Thick soups should be reheated gently; good idea to put a layer of stock or water in soup pot and then slowly "soften" over low heat until liquified, and then return to boil; bring clear soups up to a full boil.
4. Clear soup (broth, bouillon, consommé, clear vegetable soups); thick soups (purée, cream, bisque) and thick vegetable and special soups (cold soups, gazpacho, broscht).
5. Give additional color, texture, and visual appeal.
6. Rich flavor, discernible body, pleasing aroma, and rich color.
7. Broth or stock is blended with ground meat, egg whites, mireopoix, tomatoes, and aromatics, brought to a boil (proteins coagulate to form a raft), simmered gently until all impurities are captured in the raft, and then carefully strained.
8. Perfectly clear, rich-tasting, and distinct and appropriate flavor.

9. Vegetables should have clear, natural colors with no graying; vegetables should not be cooked to shreds; soup should have good flavor, color, and body; will not be as clear as either broth or consommé.
10. By simmering vegetables in a prepared velouté or by following method described on page 259.
11. Purée vegetables and return to soup; use arrowroot or cornstarch; roux.
12. Texture and consistency of heavy cream, with good fresh flavor.
13. Thicker and slightly coarser texture than cream soups, but liquid enough to pour readily from a ladle; appropriate and discernible flavor.
14. They originally were soups made of game thickened with crusts of bread or dry biscuits; may have had a garnish of crayfish. Eventually came to be associated almost exclusively with seafood, thickened with rice (though roux tends to give a better, more stable product that doesn't break down). Today, bisques are also made with vegetables, such as yellow squash or tomato.
15. Thick, smooth, with very slightly grainy texture.
16. Chowders (made with potatoes), gumbos (made with dark roux, okra, gumbo file), minestrone (pasta, beans), garbure (made by pureeing ingredients, usually including cabbage or potatoes).
17. Cream soups are chilled and served cold; based on a purée of raw or cooked ingredients, with consistency adjusted by adding a cold liquid and serving very cold.
18. Serve hot soups very hot in hot bowls; the thinner the soup, the hotter it should be when it leaves the kitchen. Serve cold soups very cold in chilled bowls (or other containers).

What Went Wrong?

1. Allowed to boil during clarification, or not allowed to simmer long enough.
2. Used too much thickener; didn't add enough stock; didn't stir frequently enough during preparation; didn't switch to another pot at the very first hint that the soup might be burning on the bottom.

Sauces

	Matching	Multiple Choice	True/False
1.	g	b	T
2.	h	a	T
3.	d	e	F
4.	a	e	F
5.	f	d	T
6.	b		
7.	i		
8.	e		
9.	j		
10.	c		

Fill in the Blank

1. butter
2. poached
3. Béchamel
4. bitterness or acidity
5. Jus lié

Discussion

1. See page 296.
2. Sauce should suit style of service; it should suit cooking technique; and flavor should be appropriate to the food.
3. They believe it makes a more stable sauce.
4. Demi-glace, velouté, béchamel, tomato (some include hollandaise as well).
5. Refer to evaluating quality section for each sauce:
   a. Demi-glace, page 299.
   b. Velouté, pages 302–3.
   c. Béchamel, pages 305.
   d. Tomato, pages 306–7.
   e. Hollandaise, page 309.
   f. Beurre blanc, page 313.
6. In a bain-marie in warm water, in a vacuum bottle.
7. Coulis, salsa, relish, compotes, and vinaigrettes.

8. Softened butter mixed with desired aromatic ingredients; used as a sauce for grilled items, or tossed with vegetables, pasta, etc.
9. Demi-glace is a sauce made by reducing Espagnole and browning sauce to half original volume; glace de viande is a remouillage reduced until it is a thick syrup that can be sliced when cold.
10. Consult specific sauces:
    1. Espagnole, page 298.
    2. Demi-glace, page 299.
    c. Velouté, pages 301–2
    d. Béchamel, page 304
    e. Tomato, page 306
    f. Hollandaise, page 308
    g. Jus lié, page 311
    h. Beurre blanc, pages 312–13

What Went Wrong?

1. Sauce may have cooled too much, or flame might be out under pan; slightly increase the heat. Also may have added all the butter that can be incorporated.
2. Sauce has broken, probably because it is too hot; perhaps the eggs were allowed to cook to too high a temperature, or perhaps the butter is too hot to add to the eggs. Remove from heat, add a small amount of cold water, and continue to beat. The sauce may become smooth, and in that case it is fine to continue with preparation. If this doesn't work, try bringing additional egg yolks to correct consistency and temperature, and then gradually incorporate the broken hollandaise.

Dry-heat Cooking
without Fats or Oils

	Matching	Multiple Choice	True/False
1.	d	b	F
2.	m	a	T
3.	k	c	T
4.	c	d	F
5.	g	e	T
6.	j		
7.	b		
8.	f		
9.	a		
10.	h		
11.	l		
12.	i		
13.	e		

Fill in the Blanks

1. "blue"
2. lower, carry-over cooking
3. instant-reading thermometer
4. white meats, game birds
5. just done

Discussion

1. Proper cuts, and determining doneness correctly.
2. Tender cuts with natural marbling. Will not toughen during contact with intense, dry heat; lack of tough connective tissue allows them to cook quickly.
3. Smoky, slightly charred flavor.
4. Broiling above, grilling below.
5. Pan-broiling is cooking in a dry pan, with all juices; rendered fats poured off immediately. Barbecuing may be roasted in a pit (traditional), grilled and basted with barbecue sauce, or cooked in a barbecue sauce in a pot.
6. To add flavor and perhaps some moisture in the form of oil.

7. To allow more than one type of doneness (or food item) to be prepared so that they can be easily identified during service.
8. Place meat on grill and let cook long enough for rods to sear the meat; turn 90 degrees onto a new spot so that marks from rods cross.
9. Refer to material on pages 345–46.
10. Flavor, appearance, and texture.
11. Refer to short form on page 346.
12. Roasted foods are cooked in a cabinet filled with hot air (oven). Grilling involves direct heat, roasting is indirect.
13. Roasted item is pierced with a spit, suspended over a heat source (with a drip pan), and turned to roast evenly.
14. Covering meat with thin sheets of fat, to baste during cooking and prevent meat from drying out.
15. See figures on page 348, and description.
16. Jus, jus lié, and pan gravy.
17. Heat held in item continues to cook it; steamship will hold a great deal of heat and may continue to cook longer and gain more degrees internal temperature. Quail is small and will lose heat rapidly, so carry-over cooking isn't as big a factor (though it is still important).
18. Add flavor to drippings for sauce.
19. Allow juices to redistribute, complete carry-over cooking, and prepare sauce. Most of the juices would run out of the meat onto the cutting board.
20. See short form on page 350.
21. Instant-reading thermometer.
22. Flavor, appearance, and texture.
23. Butter roasting. White meats, poultry, and game birds.
24. Flavor for meat as well as gravy.
25. Refer to short form on page 353.
26. To develop flavor and color.
27. Instant-reading thermometer (internal temperature is guide).
28. Flavor, appearance, and texture.
29. Foods are tender, with a deep flavor; some foods prepared by these methods (e.g., duck) may not commonly be prepare at home; healthful.

What Went Wrong?

1. Cooked too long, at too high a temperature; might have required barding. Mirepoix and drippings may have been allowed to burn; they should not have been used for the sauce.
2. Breast meat might be tender enough to cook by grilling, but legs would require longer cooking and are usually roasted.

Dry-heat Cooking with Fats and Oils

	Matching	Multiple Choice	True/False
1.	k	b	T
2.	f	e	T
3.	b	c	T
4.	g	d	T
5.	i	d	T
6.	d		
7.	c		
8.	j		
9.	e		
10.	h		
11.	a		

Fill in the Blank

1. 350°F
2. Weak flavor
3. sautéing
4. small; large
5. strong golden

Discussion

1. Naturally tender.
2. Captures flavor lost from food to pan, introduces flavor of its own, and adds moisture.
3. Stir-frying.
4. Cut into appropriate size, remove gristle and silverskin, and dust with flour (optional).
5. Develop flavor, rapid loss of juices to pan, and could stew instead of sauté.
6. Able to reach high temperatures without breaking down.
7. Same as for grilled meats (touch, appearance).
8. See short form on page 392.
9. Flavor, color, and texture.
10. White, golden, or amber exterior for white meats; red, deep-brown exterior for red meats.
11. Food is cut into small pieces, which is a form of tenderization.

12. Peanut oil for high smoking point and flavor is traditional choice, but any oil that can reach high temperatures without breaking down can be used.
13. Spices, herbs, mushrooms, vegetable garnish, sauce, and thickener.
14. Dilute a small amount of arrowroot or cornstarch in a cold liquid, add to stir-fry, and return to boil; should just coat and give glossy appearance to other items.
15. Lessen spattering and form good crust.
16. See short form on page 394.
17. Same as for sautéed foods, see page 393.
18. Sautéing uses a small amount of oil, product usually not coated, and sauce made directly in pan from rendered drippings; pan-frying uses a greater amount of oil (cover product by ¼ to ½ usually), generally coat product with standard breading or batter, and sauce made separately.
19. Cooking method does not create a flavorful fond, too much oil in pan.
20. Able to reach high temperature without breaking down.
21. Refer to diagram on page 395; item is coated in flour, egg wash, and then breadcrumbs. Gives protection as well as an interesting texture.
22. Stuffing expands during cooking, and could burst out.
23. Allow coating to dry and firm.
24. Become sticky and mat together.
25. ¼ to ½ way up the side.
26. Faint haze or shimmer on surface of oil.
27. To prevent food from absorbing oil and crust from becoming soggy.
28. Could pierce food and release juices from item into oil.
29. If it is too thick.
30. Outside golden and firm, juices show only a thread of pink, and slight amount of give when pressed.
31. Flavor, color, and texture.
32. Refer to short form on page 397.
33. Deep-fat-fried foods are completely submerged in hot oil.
34. Protection from intense heat of hot oil, and for texture contrast.
35. Refer to material on page 398.
36. Vegetable oils.
37. List found on pages 398–99.
38. Remove bones, skin, fat, gristle, silverskin, and shells, cut into appropriate shape, and bread if desired.
39. Neutral flavor, color, and high smoking point.
40. Surface will not form crust, could become soggy and soaked with oil, and may not cook properly.
41. Usually will rise to the surface of the oil.
42. Flavor, color, and texture.
43. Refer to short form on page 400.

What Went Wrong?

1. Oil not hot enough, pieces too large, coating applied too thickly, not cooked long enough.
2. Oil was old; may have been salting foods over oil, putting very wet foods such as frozen french fries with crystals of ice into oil; hadn't changed oil or filtered it recently; or oil was probably used to prepare fish at some point. The fryolater is often turned on first thing in the morning and left on all day, at 400°F. Need to replace oil, and then follow steps to maintain quality.
3. A cut other than tenderloin has probably been retrieved in error; eye of the round looks similar to a trimmed tenderloin in some ways and might have been close enough to fool the apprentice. Only naturally tender foods such as a tenderloin should be sautéed; tougher cuts are best prepared by braising or stewing.

Moist-heat Cooking

	Matching	Multiple Choice	True/False
1.	d	d	T
2.	e	b	F
3.	b	a	T
4.	f	e	T
5.	a	b or c	F
6.	c		

Fill in the Blank

1. Steamed foods
2. as the sauce
3. à la minute
4. constant, moderate
5. simmering

Discussion

1. No seal formed by contact with hot pan or oil to create flavor.
2. Retain natural juices, and introduce additional flavor.
3. Water-soluble nutrients are not drawn off.
4. Naturally tender foods that cook quickly, especially fish and shellfish.
5. Water, stock, court bouillon, beer, wine, and tea.
6. Varies according to type of food, see page 427.
7. Flavor, appearance, and texture.
8. Refer to short form on page 427.
9. Encased in parchment; natural juices of item and aromatics turn to steam, thus cooking item.
10. Advance cooking (partial, searing, etc.).
11. Can't see them or touch them without piercing bag.
12. Flavor, appearance, and texture.
13. Refer to short form on page 430.
14. Steaming and poaching.
15. To recapture flavor and nutritional value lost from item to poaching liquid.
16. Suitable for foods cut to portion size or smaller; naturally tender and quick cooking.
17. Beurre blanc made with reduction of cuisson, vegetable-based sauces, and served in broth (cuisson with addition of garnish ingredients).

18. Flesh should appear opaque, and should be plump but firm enough to offer a little resistance; oysters and clams should "curl" slightly.
19. Flavor, color, and texture.
20. Fish was overcooked or cooked too quickly.
21. See short form on page 344.
22. Slight difference in cooking temperature. Poaching is 180-185° F, simmering is 185-200° F.
23. Foods for poaching are tender; foods for simmering are more mature, less tender.
24. Temperature should be kept close to, but not at, a true boil.
25. Vigorous action of liquid at a boil would toughen and tear apart most foods.
26. Well-developed stock or broth, court bouillon, fumet.
27. To avoid overcooking exterior, reduce flavor loss, shorten cooking time.
28. Allow for expansion of liquid without boiling over, but small enough to avoid diluting flavor in too much liquid.
29. For even cooking and proper color of finished item.
30. Creates pressure, which could increase the temperature of the liquid quickly, without being easily visible.
31. Refer to material on pages 434-5.
32. Slightly undercook them, and allow to cool directly in cooking liquid off the heat. Liquid will retain enough heat to complete cooking.
33. Flavor, appearance, texture.
34. Refer to short form on page 434.

What Went Wrong?

1. Cooked for too long at too high a temperature; might have been a good idea to cook vegetables and meat separately.
2. Steamer might have built up too much pressure; might have been cooked too long; may need to wrap the snapper to protect it during steaming; sauce may need some adjustment to compensate for the delicate flavor of steamed foods.

Combination Cooking Methods

	Matching	Multiple Choice	True/False
1.	a	c	T
2.	c	d	T
3.	g	b	F
4.	l	a	F
5.	h	c	T
6.	d		
7.	k		
8.	m		
9.	e		
10.	f		
11.	j		
12.	i		
13.	b		

Fill in the Blank

1. color, flavor
2. "winter meals"
3. more mature, less tender, more flavorful
4. moisture, flavor
5. fish, shellfish

Discussion

1. Flavorful, but too tough to be successfully prepared by dry heat technique.
2. Less liquid, lower temperature, and shorter cooking time.
3. Sear main item.
4. Braised are usually portion size or larger. Enough liquid to cover by keeping moistened throughout cooking; cover by ⅓.
5. Less tender cuts can be made tender; flavor is captured in braising liquid, which is served with main item.
6. Develop color and flavor.
7. More even temperature, and less likelihood of scorching or boiling.
8. Cooking speed must be carefully regulated; check to be sure that level of liquid is maintained and that items on bottom of pot do not scorch.

9. More mature, less tender, and more flavorful.
10. Pork, tomatoes, vegetables, thickener, and garnishes.
11. Red should be seared to deep brown color; white meat until skin begins to turn color; fish do not require searing.
12. Elevate product, flavor for sauce, and moisture.
13. Allow the sauce to reduce and coat item.
14. Consistency for sauce.
15. Strain and remove, or purée and add for thickener, or, if peeled, serve as garnish for sauce.
16. Fork tender.
17. Flavor, appearance, and texture.
18. Refer to short form on page 459.
19. Main item is portion size or smaller, often cut into mouthsize pieces, and more liquid (many exceptions to this generalization, however).
20. In general, more liquid in proportion to main item, enough to cover. There are exceptions.
21. Main item is cut into small pieces so cooking time is shorter.
22. Do not vary.
23. Blanching.
24. Bite into a piece. Should be tender.
25. Flavor, appearance, texture.
26. Release from main item of proteins, etc., that contribute body. Slow gentle cooking, reduction occurs during cooking, addition of thickeners such as flour, roux, starchy vegetables. Concentration of flavors.
27. To keep cooking methods and recipes in step with contemporary tastes.

What Went Wrong?

Probably was not properly seared; may have used weak stock in sauce; not allowed to braise long enough for flavor to develop; piece of meat may not have been as flavorful; lid may not have been removed during final portion of cooking time.

Vegetable Cookery

	Matching	Multiple Choice	True/False
1.	k	c	T
2.	d	e	F
3.	h	c	F
4.	c	b	F
5.	i	a	T
6.	e		
7.	m		
8.	l		
9.	g		
10.	b		
11.	j		
12.	a		
13.	f		

Fill in the Blank

1. market
2. Braised, stewed
3. type of vegetable; technique
4. thick skins
5. same temperature; soft

Discussion

1. Add interest to plate.
2. Stir-fry is lightly cooked and crisp; braised is tender; baked can be very tender and fluffy.
3. Try pairing new techniques with familiar vegetables.
4. Purchase good quality, and exercise care in cooking.
5. Seasonality is key; do not purchase expensive product that is shipped in from far away and that does not have full taste (usually has to be picked immature, before full development).
6. Avoid loss of flavor, texture, color, vitamins, and minerals.
7. See page 491.
8. Tough, could choke.
9. Discoloration of flesh and removal of sharp barbs.
10. Make them more palatable and digestible, and improve flavor.

11. Region in which you live, and characteristics of vegetables and of technique used.
12. Appearance and texture.
13. Holding in steam tables or directly in hot water.
14. In simmering stock or water, microwave, and sautéing in butter, cream, or sauce.
15. Cook in as little water as possible as quickly as possible.
16. See list on page 496.
17. Same concerns as for nutrient loss.
18. Cook shortest time, least liquid, and close to service as possible.
19. Blanching helps remove skin, odors, and flavors, and helps to set color; parboiling cooks to desired degree of doneness (halfway is usual).
20. Water, stock, court bouillon, and milk.
21. See explanation on page 496 and recipe on page 497.
22. Retention of nutrients, color, and texture, and is efficient and gentle.
23. Cook evenly.
24. See method page 498 and short form on page 499.
25. Natural juices in vegetable heat and steam vegetable.
26. Cook in skin if there is one (squash, potato, etc.), or covered with vented plastic to steam.
27. See method on page 500. Use highest power setting.
28. Whole, large pieces, with thick protective skins.
29. Dry, mealy, and fluffy.
30. Marinade, seasonings, and aromatics.
31. Pierce skin and rub with oil.
32. Some high-moisture vegetables can be sautéed raw; others won't cook and need to be steamed, etc., first.
33. Sautéing in whole butter to reheat, glaze, and add flavor.
34. Coating with a product such as honey or other syrup to add moisture, flavor, and sheen. One way is to cook gently in a sweetened liquid or stock, which reduces to coat and glaze; another is to toss gently in butter and syrup after cooking.
35. Sautéing is only a little cooking fat; panfrying usually has a little more and may require a coating.
36. Peel, trim, rinse, cut, blanch or parcook, bread, or coat with batter.
37. Don't have enough moisture to cook properly from raw state.
38. Tempura.
39. See method and short form on page 507.
40. Eggplant, mushrooms, summer squashes, peppers, and onions.
41. Direct heat method, but one is more similar to baking or gratinee (broiling).
42. See method on pages 507–08, short form on page 508.
43. Stew is smaller pieces; more liquid than braise.
44. See method on pages 509–10, short form on page 510.
45. Served as they are, or in timbales, custards, soufflés, and ingredients in other dishes.
46. Method and short form on page 511.

What Went Wrong?

1. Poor qualities may be due to not enough water, acids in the water, vegetable itself may have been old or immature; the water may not have been at a boil; may have been overcooked or held after cooking too long.
2. May have been cooked in water without acid.
3. Cooked in water with baking soda.

Potato Cookery

	Matching	Multiple Choice	True/False
1.	i	d	F
2.	c	a	F
3.	g	b	F
4.	d	c	F
5.	a	d	F
6.	k		
7.	l		
8.	f		
9.	e		
10.	b		
11.	h		
12.	j		

Fill in the Blank

1. russet; high; low
2. Sweet potatoes, yams
3. boiling, steaming
4. bain-marie
5. granular, dry

Discussion

1. Share several characteristics and qualities with potatoes.
2. See material on page 526.
3. Sunburn; solanine poison has concentrated. Peel away green.
4. Retain nutrients, flavor, and texture.
5. Water-soluble nutrients might have been leeched into water, retain by cooking in same water.
6. Cooked by one technique from raw to finished state. Baking, boiling, steaming.
7. Cook one way, and then finished by another; puréed potatoes, baked stuffed potatoes, and home fries.
8. Refer to method (pp. 527–28) and short form (p. 528).
9. No more steam rises from potatoes.
10. Covered loosely with damp, clean cloth and kept warm.
11. Less water introduced into potato.

12. Add aromatics.
13. Refer to method and short form (both on p. 529).
14. Same as for boiling potatoes (p. 528).
15. Russet potatoes; low moisture, have best texture after baking.
16. Parcooked potato is roasted in drippings to glaze.
17. Scrub skin, pierce, and rub with either oil or salt if desired.
18. Effect is same as steaming; skin will not crisp.
19. Refer to method (pp. 529–30) and short form (p. 530).
20. Easy to pierce with kitchen fork, flesh tender and fluffy, and fresh flavor.
21. Refer to pages 530–31.
22. Refer to page 531.
23. Easy to hold, slice well for easy portioning, and generally appealing.
24. All purpose or chefs. Retain shape, have best texture.
25. Clarified butter, vegetable oil, olive oil, rendered duck, goose, or bacon fat.
26. Refer to method (p. 532) and short form (p. 534).
27. See material on page 534.
28. Least moisture in flesh.
29. To fully cook, gelatinize starch, and ease "crunch" at service time.
30. To remove starch that could cause them to stick together.
31. Vegetable oil with neutral flavor, high smoke point.
32. Refer to method and short form (p. 535).
33. See material (p. 536).
34. Boiled, steamed, and baked in skin.
35. Breaks down texture, soupy.
36. Put boiled, dried potatoes through grinder directly into bowl of mixer.
37. Break down purée and end up with heavy, pasty consistency.
38. Refer to method (p. 536) and short form (p. 537).
39. Smooth, light in texture, and able to hold shape when dropped from a spoon. Refer to page 537.
40. Refer to method (pp. 538–39) and short form (p. 538)

What Went Wrong?

1. Potatoes were not cooked and dried properly, may not have been put through ricer, sieve, or foley mill, or may have been overworked.
2. Oil has probably begun to break down, so potatoes do not cook evenly; perhaps the potatoes were not blanched first at a lower temperature; perhaps temperature is set too high.
3. Should cook potatoes in batches of reasonable size for best texture and flavor; as they are held, they lose texture and flavor begins to get sweet.

Cooking Grains and Legumes

	Matching	Multiple Choice	True/False
1.	g	b	F
2.	e	b	T
3.	f	d	T
4.	c	c	F
5.	a	a	T
6.	d		
7.	h		
8.	b		

Fill in the Blank

1. longer
2. any of several methods; always boiled
3. digestible
4. distinctive bite
5. greater

Discussion

1. Fruit of grass; see material on page 550 regarding milling processes.
2. Major portion of grain, which holds most of the nutrients.
3. Seeds that grow in pods; available fresh and dried.
4. Complete protein, complex carbohydrates, dietary fiber, vitamins, and minerals.
5. Change flavor, develop flavor, and deactivate unpleasant or harmful substances naturally present in uncooked form.
6. Dry, away from heat, light, and moisture; may need to store whole grains under refrigeration.
7. Remove debris and moldy pieces.
8. Milled, enriched, and polished; could rinse away valuable nutrients.
9. Shorten cooking time.
10. Way legume is attached to pod; allows water to slowly enter and soften bean.
11. Short soak (bring to a boil, remove from heat, soak 1 hour); overnight soak in cold water.
12. Refer to material on page 552.
13. Refer to method (p. 553) and short form (p. 555).

14. Toughens them and lengthens cooking time.
15. Tender to the bite (see material on p. 553 for some exceptions and further description).
16. Couscous, possibly rice.
17. Pot for preparing couscous (stew on bottom, steam couscous in perforated top).
18. Refer to method (p. 555) and short form (p. 556).
19. Soak in tepid water.
20. Tender to the bite, easy to separate and fluff with fork.
21. Grain heated in pan, then liquid added, brought to simmer, and cooked covered until grains are tender; easy to separate.
22. Stock and water, perhaps with the addition of vegetable juices (but may affect total cooking time).
23. Lengthen it; if there is too much, it may never get very soft, no matter how long it is cooked.
24. Gelatinizes starches so that they remain separate (do not clump) when done cooking.
25. Refer to method (p. 557) and short form (p. 559) and photo sequence 24-4.
26. Tender, but retain some texture; grains separate easily.
27. Short grain.
28. Both characteristics of the type of rice (starchier) and the cooking method itself.
29. Arborio rice, broth, wine, grated parmesan cheese, and butter.
30. Last addition so that acid will not toughen the grain.
31. Refer to method (pp. 559–60), short form (p. 560), and photo sequence 24-5.
32. Cook up to the last addition of liquid, spread out to cool, and finish portion by portion.
33. Creamy, porridge-like consistency; each grain still has distinct bite.
34. Very popular, healthy, and interesting flavors and textures.

What Went Wrong?

1. Did not parch grain first, used too much liquid, or cooked too long.
2. Used wrong type of rice, not enough liquid, did not stir throughout preparation, or not cooked long enough.
3. May have added an acidic ingredient, such as tomatoes, lemon, or vinegar, too soon; beans may be old, or heat may be too low.

Cooking Pasta and Dumplings

	Matching	Multiple Choice	True/False
1.	b	d	T
2.	e	b	T
3.	g	b	T
4.	h	d	F
5.	i	a	T
6.	c		
7.	d		
8.	a		
9.	f		

Fill in the Blank

1. additional flour, less water
2. by hand, in food processor, with an electric mixer
3. resting stage; "relaxed"
4. light cream, butter-based
5. richness, color

Discussion

1. Pasta dough is stiff because of little liquid; batter has more liquid, and pours or drops from spoon easily.
2. Dry can be held in dry storage indefinitely, and has different texture and different taste; fresh is tender, easy to vary.
3. Durum, semolina, manitoba, and bread flour (any wheat flour with a high-protein content).
4. Provide richness, flavor, and color.
5. Adjust moisture content in formula to adjust for moisture in additional ingredients.
6. Steep first to release color and add along with eggs.
7. Hand, mixer, and processor.
8. Refer to method (pp. 573–75) and short forms (pp. 574–75).
9. Allow gluten to relax so that it can be rolled easily without pulling back into shape.
10. Refer to material on page 575.
11. Refer to method (pp. 575–76) and short form (p. 576).
12. Refer to method (pp. 576–77) and short form (p. 577).

13. Even cuts.
14. Hold under refrigeration for one or two days, on sheet pans coated with cornmeal, or allow to dry for longer storage in dry storage.
15. 8:1 by weight (1 gallon (4 quarts) to 1 pound of pasta).
16. Fresh cooks faster.
17. Drain, rinse in cold water to stop cooking, drain, and rub with oil.
18. See material on page 578.
19. See material on pages 578–79.
20. See material on page 579.
21. Refer method and short form (p. 578).
22. Wide variety, could be a number of different preparations.
23. Simmered, steamed, poached, baked, pan-fried, and deep-fried.
24. Through colander, scraping off board with palette knife, and using spaetzli press.
25. Refer to material on page 580.
26. Refer to material on page 580.

What Went Wrong?

1. Water was not at a full boil, or didn't stir with a fork to separate strands as it cooks; if fresh, dough may have been too wet; may not have been enough water in pot.
2. Didn't follow formula for biscuit correctly, didn't add any or enough leavener, or didn't cook properly.

Breakfast and Egg Cookery

	Matching	Multiple Choice	True/False
1.	j	c	F
2.	g	b	T
3.	d	b	T
4.	i	d	F
5.	a	a	F
6.	c		
7.	k		
8.	e		
9.	b		

Fill in the Blank

1. leached
2. infusion
3. in constant motion
4. used at once
5. cold water

Discussion

1. Refer to material on page 598.
2. Refer to material on page 598.
3. Refer to method on page 598.
4. Better appearance, yolk less likely to break, and white is neater.
5. Refer to method on page 599.
6. Cook in poaching liquid, shock and hold in cold water, reheat in simmering water, and then blot dry before service.
7. Refer to material on page 600.
8. Refer to method on page 600.
9. Rolled, flat, souffléd, or puffy.
10. Refer to method on page 601 and short form on page 603, photo sequence 26-2.
11. Refer to method on pages 602–04, short form on page 604.
12. Refer to method on page 604, short form on page 605.

13. 6 to 8 eggs per quart of liquid.
14. Prepared and flavored base, beaten egg whites.
15. Timing.
16. Refer to method on pages 606–07 and short form on page 608.
17. Type of batter used.
18. Refer to material on page 610.
19. Granola, corn flakes, sweetened, high fiber, oatmeal, porridge, bulgar, groats, grits, and cornmeal mush.
20. Cooked until crisp in pan, on griddle, in oven, or in microwave (never deep-fry).
21. Refer to material on page 611.
22. Poached or fried egg.
23. See material on page 612.
24. A beverage made by extracting flavor from roasted, ground beans with hot (190°F) water; drip, percolate, and brew.
25. Leaves an impression on guest, often the last impression.
26. According to needs and available equipment and storage space.
27. Create an infusion by pouring boiling water over leaves (loose or in bag) and steeping to desired intensity, remove leaves, and drink immediately.

What Went Wrong?

1. Used very fresh eggs (hard to peel) and may have either been overcooked or not peeled quickly enough to release gas that reacts with iron in yolk to make green ring (sulfur is the gas).
2. Eggs are old, temperature is too high, handling was too rough, or forgot to add acid to water.
3. May have been overcooked to start with or held too long on the line; may have added too much liquid to the eggs while scrambling; moisture may also be from ingredients such as mushrooms, peppers, or tomatoes.

Hors d'Oeuvre, Appetizers, and Salads

	Matching	Multiple Choice	True/False
1.	l	a	T
2.	f	d	T
3.	a	e	T
4.	n	a	T
5.	i	b	T
6.	c		
7.	k		
8.	j		
9.	m		
10.	d		
11.	g		
12.	e		
13.	o		
14.	b		
15.	h		

Fill in the Blank

1. Beluga, osetra, sevruga
2. acidity, oils
3. knife
4. appetizers
5. Crudités

Discussion

1. Availability, seasonality, budget, and creativity.
2. Fresh, appealing flavor and texture, small, and easy to eat in one bite.
3. Refer to material on pages 630-31.
4. Chopped hard-cooked egg, onion, capers, lemon juice, buttered bread, or blini.
5. Refer to material on page 631.
6. Keep portion size appropriate, do not overwhelm with herbs and spices, and keep presentation in mind.

7. Health concerns, increased availability of locally grown "wild" greens, influences from various countries and cuisines, and climate.
8. Flavors and textures.
9. Refer to material on pages 634–37, including photo sequences.
10. ⅓ fluid ounce of dressing to 1 ounce of greens.
11. Dress just before service; may assemble salads on sheet trays, spray with dressing, and transfer to plates.
12. Appetizer, entrée, or side dish.
13. Refer to material on page 638.
14. Mellow, not too sharp (too much vinegar) or too oily.
15. Thick, creamy, balanced flavor, smooth, and hint of sharpness to brighten flavor.
16. Refer to method on pages 640–41 and short form on page 641.
17. Refer to method and short from on page 639.
18. Refer to method on pages 639–40 and short form on page 639.

What Went Wrong?

1. Ingredients may not have been at room temperature; may be incorporating too much oil too quickly; may not have used enough egg yolks to absorb quantity of oil; may not have correct balance of ingredients; mixture may be getting either too hot or too cold.
2. Cleaning greens too far in advance; holding in water or at room temperature (too warm, humidity wrong); adding dressing too soon, causing greens to wilt; adding too much dressing overall.

Charcuterie and Garde-manger

	Matching	Multiple Choice	True/False
1.	h	c	T
2.	o	a	F
3.	a	c	F
4.	k	e	F
5.	m	d	T
6.	c		
7.	f		
8.	p		
9.	d		
10.	g		
11.	n		
12.	e		
13.	i		
14.	b		
15.	l		
16.	j		

Fill in the Blank

1. true emulsion
2. dominant meat
3. 20 percent
4. heavy cream
5. sodium nitrate

Discussion

1. Refer to material on page 666.
2. Sanitation and proper emulsion won't form.
3. Grind through coarse die, then medium die, then (optional) fine die, and then (optional) food processor.
4. A binder, usually made of starchy ingredients or cream, and egg yolks.
5. Clarified and strengthened broth used to coat items, to prevent drying and to add color and sheen.
6. Refer to material on pages 667-68.

7. Refer to material on pages 666–67.
8. Refer to method (p. 669), photo sequence 28-1, and short form (p. 670).
9. Refer to method (p. 670), photo sequence 28-2, and short form (p. 670).
10. Refer to method (pp. 672–74), photo sequence 28-4, and short form (p. 674).
11. Refer to method (pp. 670–72), photo sequence 28-3, and short form (p. 672).
12. Refer to method (p. 674), photo sequence 28-5, and short form (p. 676).
13. A dumpling made from forcemeat; sample to test quality of forcemeat, garnish for soup, and appetizer.
14. Poached, grilled, fried, or baked.
15. Campagne is generally without crust, en croute is with.
16. Refer to method on page 681.
17. Originally made exclusively from poultry, and tied to retain natural shape; today, made from a variety of ingredients, including fish and vegetables. May use skin if available as casing.
18. Cure may be a dry mixture of spices, salt, and herbs used to coat item as a crust, then scraped away; brine is a liquid cure used to submerge item.
19. Hot smoking cooks item because temperature is above 145°F; cold smoking does not, because temperature in smoker is less than 100°F.
20. Cured salmon (with a dry cure) made by packing a cure on salmon fillet and letting cure for several days under weight in refrigerator (refer also to method on pp. 683–84).
21. Prepared by very gently simmering a number of meats in a broth until tender and gelatinous; allowed to cool in mold and sliced as for head cheese.

What Went Wrong?

1. May not have formed a good emulsion during preparation, as might happen if ingredients were allowed to become too warm (equipment too); may have needed a panada, or more panada than was added; may have cooked galantine at too high temperature.

Baking Mise en Place

	Matching	Multiple Choice	True/False
1.	c	c	F
2.	e	c	T
3.	f	a	T
4.	i	b	T
5.	j	d	F
6.	h	d	T
7.	b		T
8.	a		F
9.	g		F
10.	d		T

Fill in the Blank

1. docking
2. bloomed
3. Caramelization
4. the backbone of baked goods
5. simple syrup
6. after the ingredients are properly scaled

Discussion

1. See page 717 for steps in tempering chocolate.
2. As a coating, by dipping items in chocolate, or pouring the tempered chocolate over them; pour it onto a marble slab, work with a spatula until it loses glossy appearance, and then cut into shapes; pipe tempered chocolate out through parchment cones to make decorations, with or without a stencil.
3. For delicate items, coat liberally with shortening, a combination of shortening and flour, and greased parchment paper. Lean doughs are usually baked in pans coated with cornmeal; angel food cakes and chiffon cakes in ungreased tube pans.
4. Ensures accuracy and consistency when preparing ingredients to mix into batters; once dough is mixed, scaling assures that enough, but not too much, dough or batter is placed in the pan so that it will bake properly. Items could have wrong texture, taste, or appearance, or they might burn or never bake properly.
5. Dilute in a small amount of cold liquid before adding to a hot liquid. Translucent effect can be achieved.

6. Fat surrounds the long strands of batter or dough so that the finished produce has a "shorter" crumb and a more tender texture. The more fully incorporated the shortening ingredient is, the more tender the overall finished item (e.g., a cake that has the butter completely blended into the batter is more tender and less flaky than a pie dough that has the fat only minimally worked into the flour).

What Went Wrong?

1. Gelatin was not properly softened and melted before adding it to another liquid.
2. Egg whites were used to replace egg yolks. Egg whites are strengtheners, while egg yolks provide a tenderizing effect.
3. Double acting baking powder was used and the dough was allowed to become too hot as it sat near the griddle, or the dough was not properly scaled before it was placed in the pan.

Yeast Doughs

	Matching	Multiple Choice	True/False
1.	c	a	F
2.	a	c	F
3.	g	a	T
4.	i	b	F
5.	b	d	T
6.	d		F
7.	h		F
8.	e		T
9.	j		T
10.	f		F

Fill in the Blank

1. wild yeast spores
2. rye, oat, or pumpernickel; wheat flour
3. high temperatures
4. slowed down or inhibited; killed by them
5. helps to control the growth of the yeast

Discussion

1. Good aroma, color, texture, and flavor (see p. 730 for full description).
2. Good impression on guest; aroma is pleasant and has good associations for guest; can be dovetailed with other work in kitchen, as when baker comes early in the morning when no other staff is around; needs for simple baking are few and can usually be accommodated in a smaller kitchen without buying special equipment and tools.
3. Allows steam to escape so that dough does not burst during baking.
4. Allows dough to bake evenly, get good rise, even has an effect on the "crumb" of the dough; also looks better and more appealing to the guest.
5. Distributes yeast evenly, releases carbon dioxide gas from dough, and evens out temperature of dough.

What Went Wrong?

1. Improperly mixed; too much salt, not enough dough in pan; dough was either proofed too long or not long enough; see chart on page 730.
2. Not enough salt; proofed too long and allowed to remain too warm for too long during rising and shaping; dough too stiff; used "green" flour or not enough sugar.
3. The bread dough was allowed to proof too long.

Quickbreads, Cakes, and Other Batters

	Matching	Multiple Choice	True/False
1.	a	c	F
2.	d	d	F
3.	g	d	T
4.	b	a	T
5.	h	c	F
6.	i		F
7.	c		T
8.	j		T
9.	f		T
10.	e		F

Fill in the Blank

1. air tunnels and pockets after baking
2. a chemical leavener
3. straight mixing method
4. angel food cakes, chiffon cakes, genoise, sponge cakes, and jelly roll cakes
5. paddle attachment

Discussion

1. Crust is dark, cake shrinks too much (is small), and may burst on top; cake will become stale rapidly.
2. Eggs, butter, and sugar.
3. Cakes have more sugar than other formulas, possibly because of the use of high-ratio shortening that can be supersaturated with sugar; additional sugar keeps cake moister longer and prevents rapid staling due to hydroscopic nature of sugar. When mixing, all of flour and shortening is combined first, along with half of liquid; remaining liquid is added 2 or 3 parts; total mixing time should be no longer than about 10 minutes.
4. See pages 748–749.
5. See page 744.
6. See pages 740–741.

What Went Wrong.

1. Batter was improperly prepared; did not have enough flour; used too much leavener; used wrong type of flour; failed to properly drain and dry fruit.
2. Batter was improperly mixed; stiff; included too much leavener; had too few eggs; baked at a temperature that was too low.

Pastry Doughs and Cookies

	Matching	Multiple Choice	True/False
1.	j	d	F
2.	e	c	F
3.	h	c	T
4.	b	a	F
5.	i	b	F
6.	a		T
7.	f		T
8.	c		T
9.	d		F
10.	g		F

Fill in the Blank

1. phyllo, filo, and strudel
2. shortbread
3. mealy
4. 3-2-1 dough flour, fat, and water
5. turn

Discussion

1. Bar cookies, drop cookies, bagged or spritz cookies, sheet cookies, ice box cookies. Served as a part of dessert, at a reception, or with coffee and tea.
2. The degree to which fat is incorporated into batter or dough will affect the final texture. The more thoroughly it is blended in, the more tender and crumbly. The less, the more flaky.
3. Thaw slowly overnight if frozen; keep sheets covered with damp toweling and plastic when not being worked on; brush lightly or spray with oil or butter and/or scatter with crumbs to keep sheets separate during baking so that finished product is flaky.
4. Prepare dough and let rise; prepare roll-in so that it has same consistency as dough. Roll out dough into large rectangle. Cover two-thirds with roll-in (leave margin) and fold (like a letter); weld seams. Continue making folds and roll out, as described on pages 769–70.
5. Flaky pie dough leaves fat in large pieces, creating sheets and flaky texture. Mealy pie dough has fat more thoroughly worked into dough so that final texture is crumbly and mealy. Both use the same ratio for ingredients; difference is in mixing method.

6. A tart pan is usually not as deep as a pie plate and has straight sides and only one crust on the bottom; a pie is usually baked in a pan with flared sides and is deeper than a tart pan, frequently has a double-crust.

What Went Wrong?

1. Used insufficient shortening in dough; not enough (or too much) liquid and wrong type of flour; may have been mixed too long.
2. Used too much shortening in or overworked dough; baked at wrong temperature (too low or too high); bottom heat in the oven may not have been sufficient; filling may have been too acidic or too hot when added to crust; allowed to boil during baking; made with either too much or too little sugar; or crusts may have been improperly sealed.

Dessert Sauces, Creams, and Frozen and Fruit Desserts

	Matching	Multiple Choice	True/False
1.	g	b	T
2.	c	a	T
3.	e	c	T
4.	b	b	T
5.	f	d	T
6.	a		F
7.	h		F
8.	d		T
9.	j		T
10.	i		F

Fill in the Blank

1. Bavarian cream, baked custard, flavored, used as a mousse, and made into ice cream
2. egg yolks, hot syrup, flavoring, and softened butter
3. mousse
4. baked meringues, cookie doughs
5. frosting or filling

Discussion

1. Churning action introduces air into mixture and prevents it from becoming a solid lump for ice cream. Also, sugar and high fat ingredients such as cream do not freeze solid the same way that water does.
2. German is made with pastry cream and butter; Italian with a meringue made from egg whites and hot sugar syrup and butter; French with egg yolks, hot syrup, and butter; and Swiss with custard sauce and butter.
3. Layer cake is sliced and brushed with syrup, or layers of baked meringue or cookies are baked; crumbs are brushed away; layers are filled and then stacked; frosting is applied evenly; and decorations are applied.
4. Caramel, butterscotch, fruit such as berry coulis, warm dried fruit compotes, and chocolate (ganache).

What Went Wrong?

1. Too much sugar in syrup.
2. Too many egg yolks in proportion to cream.